D1416314

PRAISE FOR

AMERICA'S SURVIVAL GUIDE

"*America's Survival Guide* by Michael Warren describes with detail and passion the dangers that come from abandoning the 'First Principles' upon which this nation was founded. But this important book offers more than a diagnosis and despair, it presents a reasoned program for restoring the U.S. Constitution its proper place at the center of American society and government. *America's Survival Guide* draws on history, politics and education to make a powerful case for freedom and fighting for it."

JOHN ENGLER, FORMER GOVERNOR OF MICHIGAN AND CURRENT PRESIDENT AND
CEO OF THE NATIONAL ASSOCIATION OF MANUFACTURERS

"Judge Warren has written a deeply informative history of the philosophical origins of American freedom. *America's Survival Guide* is a challenge to present day Americans to love freedom, as did our forebears, or face the loss of it. If you want to know why it is just as vital to fight complacency about freedom . . . as it is to fight the forces that attacked us on 9/11, read this book."

JUDGE ANDREW P. NAPOLITANO,
FOX NEWS CHANNEL, SENIOR JUDICIAL ANALYST

"*America's Survival Guide* is a bold and insightful work that should be taken seriously by those concerned with the future of America. We ignore it at our peril."

CONGRESSMAN JOE KNOLLENBERG

"A comprehensive *tour de force* of what is going wrong with our republic and how to make it right. It does not matter if you come from the ideological left, right or straight-down the middle – this book is worth reading if you love America and cherish our freedom."

TOM WATKINS, FORMER SUPERINTENDENT OF PUBLIC INSTRUCTION AND
DIRECTOR OF THE DEPARTMENT OF MENTAL HEALTH FOR THE STATE OF MICHIGAN

"Judge Warren eloquently describes the amnesia affecting our democratic republic. The historical section provides a rich teaching resource for American history and civics. A must read for teachers and students alike."

AMY BLOOM, OAKLAND SCHOOLS HISTORY/SOCIAL STUDIES CONSULTANT

"Michael Warren is the Paul Revere of the 21st century, warning of an invasion of the American spirit that threatens to eviscerate the country's founding principles and rot the nation from within. He documents the historical illiteracy that is truly dumbing down the future of America, its children. It's time for America to answer this intellectual and spiritual call-to-arms."

RICHARD BURR, THE DETROIT NEWS, ASSOCIATE EDITOR, EDITORIAL PAGE

"Judge Michael Warren has filled these pages with some of the best ideas emerging from our history – ideas that he argues form the very foundations of America's political and social life. Meant to stir us from a civic lethargy, Warren provokes as he educates. Indeed, there is much here worth talking about, arguing over, and acting upon. Whether you agree or disagree with him, Judge Warren has given policy makers, teachers and students a powerful picture of America's intellectual past to guide the present as we shape the future."

BOB BAIN, UNIVERSITY OF MICHIGAN, ASSOCIATE PROFESSOR

"This book should be required reading in our public high schools. It is well-written, gathers the reader's interest by establishing the danger that America is in, and provides an excellent discussion of our founding principles and why they are important. Michael Warren deserves high praise for his efforts in rescuing us from the disaster of ignorance of what it means to be an American."

GARY WOLFRAM, HILLSDALE COLLEGE,
GEORGE MUNSON PROFESSOR OF POLITICAL ECONOMY

"Our democracy's survival rests upon our transmitting to each new generation the political vision of liberty and equality that unites us as Americans. Jefferson stated it best when he said, 'If we expect in a state of civilization to be ignorant and free, we expect what never was and never will be.' Michael Warren is a true modern patriot whose efforts in education are one way to build a strong democracy for our future."

J. KELLI SWEET, MICHIGAN COUNCIL FOR THE SOCIAL STUDIES,
EXECUTIVE DIRECTOR

"Finally! Someone addresses the concerns many of us Americans have and approaches them from an apolitical point of view. Michael Warren speaks from a position of reasoned authority and examines the U.S. landscape from politics, to the courts, to the schools, to the media. This expert on law and education, does not leave the reader in a state of depression but rather offers potential solutions that all can embrace. This is a book for all who hope for a better future in our country, and that should include all of us."

FRANK BECKMANN, WJR 760 AM

AMERICA'S
SURVIVAL GUIDE

*How to Stop America's Impending Suicide by
Reclaiming Our First Principles and History*

www.AmericasSurvivalGuide.com

MICHAEL WARREN

AMERICA'S
SURVIVAL GUIDE

*How to Stop America's Impending Suicide by
Reclaiming Our First Principles and History*

www.AmericasSurvivalGuide.com

Mill City Press, Inc.
Minneapolis, Minnesota

For more information contact, Mill City Press, Inc., 212 3rd Avenue North, Suite 570, Minneapolis, MN 55401
or info@millcitypress.net

www.millcitypress.net

Cover and Interior Design by Elizabeth Wargo

ISBN 1-934248-31-2
ISBN 978-1-934248-31-7
LCCN 2007929589

Printed in the United States of America

Orders: www.AmericasSurvivalGuide.com

To the Founding Fathers, to whom I owe the past and present;
and for my daughters, Leah and Lily, to whom I entrust the future.

ACKNOWLEDGEMENTS

This work would not be possible without the support and patience of my wife Shannon. I must also acknowledge those who have provided extremely helpful comments, recommendations, and suggestions during the course of this project, most especially Amy Bloom (who read and provided thoughtful comments to several drafts) and Bob Bain. Michael Brady, Greg Reid, and Michael DeBruyn also served as superb sounding boards. My profuse thanks to those luminaries who made the time in their very busy schedules to both review the book and provide supportive comments. Special thanks to Robert Hallmark. The professionals at Mill City Press, especially Mark Levine, have been invaluable. Brian Downing served as an excellent editor.

CONTENTS

PREFACE

I confess. I have spent over a decade researching, writing, and revising this work. I have done so because I fear that the light of liberty is slowly being extinguished.

Thankfully, the book is finally published. I expect that the ostentatious, and somewhat irreverent, title of the work has raised some eyebrows. Good. As a nation we are asleep and decaying. Time to awake or lose everything. I, for one, am not willing to fade quietly into the night. Join me.

INTRODUCTION

The Independence of America, considered merely as a separation from England, would have been a matter of but little
importance, had it not been accompanied by a Revolution
in the principles and practice of Governments. She made a
stand, not for herself only, but for the world, and looked beyond the advantages herself could receive. Thomas Paine,
The Rights of Man (1792).

Happily for America, happily we trust for the whole human
race, [the Founding Fathers] pursued a new and more noble
course. They accomplished a revolution which has no parallel in the annals of human society. They reared the fabrics
of governments which have no model on the face of the
globe. James Madison, *The Federalist, No. 14* (1788).

America is slowly committing suicide. That we are doing so is not obvious. Indeed, most might consider this conclusion to be myopic if not outright outlandish in light of our apparent economic, cultural, and military
dominance in the world. Certainly most consider America to be all but invul-
nerable, and that whatever serious threats we face will arise from outside our
borders. In fact, one casually examining the title of this work might expect it
to focus on militant Islamist terrorists or the awakening Asian giants China
and India.

Contrary to popular wisdom, the most serious threat to America does not spring from overseas. Because the threat is from within, it is much more subtle. This peril lingers and silently brews under the surface. Virulent, this contagion slowly spreads – infecting ever greater parts of the body politic. Like a phantom, the crisis is everywhere – but elusive. We vaguely sense there is something amiss, but are unable to pinpoint it. When our attention is captured by the news entertainment of the day, we put aside our unease. After all, there is no big event to follow. There are no lurid details of deaths or sexual affairs to draw our curiosity. This menace eludes capture on video; it is not easily emblazoned on the headlines of newspapers.

At the core of this menace is something exceedingly simple. In our cyber-speed lives, what should be open and obvious is hidden. This is so because the danger involves a crisis of the American spirit. In short, there is widespread, pure, and unadulterated ignorance and disdain of the founding principles and history of America. Our self-evident truths have become neither. This state of affairs imperils our very survival; and these are self-inflicted wounds – the very definition of suicide.

This book is written with the perhaps naïve hope that our leaders and citizens will awaken. In essence, this work is intended to serve as a "one stop, full-service" primer to sound the alarm about the impending suicide of America and to outline the means to stop it. Part I documents the severe depth of the challenge we face by surveying the overwhelming evidence of the rampant ignorance and disdain of American history and our First Principles. Part II clearly and concisely reviews America's First Principles, and how the First Principles are the foundation of the American Revolution, the United States Constitution, and the great civil rights movements. Part III offers specific recommendations to stop America's suicide. These recommendations include education, legal, media, holiday, nonprofit, and political reform. Each Part has its own independent value, and in some sense stands alone. Together, they provide what we need to stop us from drinking our collective hemlock.

Part I
America's Impending Suicide

At what point then is the approach of danger to be expected? I answer, if it ever reach us, it must spring up amongst us. It cannot come from overbroad. If destruction be our lot, we must ourselves be its author and finisher. As a nation of freemen, we must live through all time, or die by suicide. Abraham Lincoln, *Address to the Young Men's Lyceum of Springfield, Illinois* (1838).

An ignorant people will never live long under a free government. They will soon become slaves, or run into anarchy. Zabiel Adams, *An Election Sermon* (1782).

Chapter 1
Ignorance and Disdain:
The Threat from Within

Only lay down true principles, and adhere to them inflexibly. Do not be frightened into their surrender by the alarms of the timid, or the croakings of wealth against the ascendancy of the people. . . .

A departure from principle in one instance becomes a precedent for a second; that second for a third; and so on, till the bulk of the society is reduced to be mere automatons of misery, to have no sensibilities left but for sin and suffering. Thomas Jefferson, *Letter to Samuel Kercheval* (1816).

❋   America was founded on First Principles

❋   Striving to fulfill our First Principles has made America a free, just, and great nation

❋   Politicians, the media, educators, academics, the legal profession, and the general public generally ignore or even attack our First Principles and history

❋   By ignoring and denigrating our First Principles and history, America is slowly committing suicide

❋   Only by reinvigorating our understanding of America's First Principles and history can we survive and prosper

---

We are the first, perhaps the only nation that holds as self-evident truths that all men and women are created equal and are endowed by their Creator with certain unalienable rights; and that governments are instituted to protect those rights and derive their just powers from the consent of the governed. Stated differently, America was founded on certain First Principles:

(i)   The rule of law;

(ii)   The recognition and protection of the unalienable rights of individuals;

(iii)   The equality of individuals;

(iv)   The Social Compact (*i.e.*, that governments are instituted by the people and derive their just powers from the consent of the governed); and

(v)   The protection of unalienable rights as the legitimate purpose and limit of government (*i.e.*, the government must have the authority and strength to protect the unalienable rights of the people, but only have such power as is necessary to fulfill that purpose).

Our *Declaration of Independence* explains that these foundational ideas were the philosophical underpinning of the American Revolution. Once independence was secured, the Founding Fathers labored to ensure that the Constitution became the living embodiment of a government based on these First Principles.

The Founding Fathers often referred to America as a great experiment in government and society. The experiment was to determine whether a government established on First Principles could survive and prosper. Fortunately for their posterity and the world, the experiment was an unparalleled success.

Indeed, guided by these First Principles, America became not only a free and just nation, but the exemplar for the world. Driven by the aspiration to fulfill our First Principles, the country at great cost abolished slavery, enfranchised women, reformed electoral politics, and enacted other major political reforms. Enabled by our First Principles, free men and women sparked scientific, social, and economic innovations and movements profoundly changing the world. Despite our shortcomings, America is a singularly exceptional nation – and that exceptionalism arises, in large measure, from our embracing the First Principles and striving to make them reality.

Armed with these First Principles, America also swept away the Old World order, conquered fascism, and won the Cold War. Much to the chagrin of his critics, in 1981 President Ronald Reagan boldly predicted at the University of Notre Dame that America would not only contain communism, but transcend it. Fulfilling that prophesy, America overcame communism with the fruits of a free society: a booming economy, break-through technology, a strong military, and a spirited people united to maintain their freedom. The people, building upon the strong foundation of a just and free government, reveal – and revel in – the marvels of a free society. Freedom of religion and a deeply religious people; free enterprise and competition; vigorous free thought and creativity; the drive to succeed and charity; the spirit of adventure and discovery; invention and innovation; daring risk taking and rewards; and the opportunity to succeed and advance based on merit are all critical components of American society that flourishes because of our adherence to the First Principles.

Despite our shortcomings, America has no superior in manufacturing, design, engineering, agriculture, commerce, finance, military might, volunteerism, research, technology, medicine, entertainment, media, sports, and literature. America is the most wealthy and powerful nation in history, and its greatness springs from the work of free citizens. Greatness, however, is not a reason in itself to follow the First Principles. After all, "greatness" in the eyes of some may also be achieved through military junta, totalitarianism, or communism. The First Principles are an end in themselves because they preserve the unalienable rights of each individual by creating a free and just society – the true purpose of government.

Perhaps as important as our past achievements is our everlasting desire to improve our society. This unceasing striving for perfection separates us from all other nations in history – it is as much the striving as the doing. We *seek* to be a free and just people. In struggling to fulfill that promise, we inspire not only ourselves but the world. Our First Principles are a beacon of light – a flame of liberty – that move our nation and the world. Echoing the sentiments of the Founding Fathers and the Gospels, President Reagan often remarked that we are a great "City on the Hill" to which billions even now aspire.

The American experiment now teeters on the brink of collapse. We have all but forgotten the exceptional nature of America. We are nourishing our freedoms on the fruits sown and nourished by our forefathers. Studies reveal that the public is ignorant of key concepts and principles of our constitutional order.[1] Despite the importance of the First Principles, our political elite, media, public, and educators have all but forgotten or rejected them.

Fashionable politicians have become adept in wrapping themselves in the flag and spouting patriotic sound-bites. Yet most political leaders do not appear to know or understand our First Principles or history. They certainly do not seriously discuss or consider them when addressing the issues of the day. Others in the political elite simply believe that our founding principles should be relegated to backwater history courses and dusty library books. Presidential and congressional campaigns engage in a broad range of topics, but almost never mention or address our First Principles. To observe that our political dialogue has degenerated into an exercise just short of name calling, is chock full of poisonous partisan wrangling, and often is nothing more than the politics of personal destruction, is to simply state the obvious. Almost by happenstance a rare leader may stumble into an argument well-grounded in our history and First Principles. Stumbling into principles and history, however, is hardly sufficient to preserve our constitutional liberties. Almost all of our current political discourse ignores our First Principles and history out of ignorance, convenience, or disdain.

Much of the mainstream media is also blissfully unaware of anything approaching history or foundational principles. Rapt by the soap opera lives of celebrities, the bizarre antics of the maladjusted, the crime of the day, the scandal of the week, the protest or gaffe of the month, and the blistering invective of politicians, the media have all but ignored serious probing of our political state of affairs. In fact, most of the media is so preoccupied with short-term attention-grabbing headlines that it completely glosses over the long-term systematic challenges facing the country. The mainstream media almost never address the historical underpinnings or processes of government, or how they are relevant to the issues of the day.

Even when presented with historic opportunities to explore America's rich history, the media choose to highlight the inane, banal, emotional, and trivial. Mainstream news coverage of watershed events such as impeachment, elections, terrorism, the Iraq and Afghanistan Wars, massive new social programs, the growing entitlement crisis, Supreme Court nominations, record-breaking trade deficits, the War on Terror, and nuclear proliferation has been and continues to be dominated by personalities, fashion, glib remarks, gossip, and a hodge-podge of ill-informed commentary. All of these events and issues presented (and some continue to present) an excellent backdrop by which to explore the meaning of the rule of law, the Social Compact, equality, unalienable rights, and the purpose and limitations of government. Most of the mainstream media has squandered the opportunity to inform and challenge the public. Coverage of our First Principles is simply verboten.

Similarly, most people are ignorant of our First Principles. Since the start of the War on Terror, crowds began to once again proudly wave the American flag and sing songs of patriotism. In fact, Americans are the most patriotic citizens of all.[2] Yet many even struggle to recall the words of *The Star Spangled Banner* – or that it is the national anthem.[3] More important, their understanding of what the flag represents and the meaning of patriotic songs are often very shallow. For example, 41% of the people appear clueless about the Bill of Rights.[4] Less than half understand that there are a hundred Senators.[5]

Although more than half of Americans can correctly identify two of the five main characters from *The Simpsons*, less than a third can correctly identify two of the major five First Amendment rights.[6] Only one in a thousand can correctly identify five of the rights protected by the First Amendment.[7] Barely half of Americans can correctly identify the three branches of government, less than half the meaning of separation of powers, and again less than half the role of the judiciary in the federal government.[8] Most Americans instinctively believe in a republican form of government, but not many understand the philosophical and historical origins that compelled the Founders to fight for and adopt such a system. Similarly, too few of our citizens understand the roles of the judiciary, legislature, and executive, and even fewer can explain how checks and balances, enumerated powers, and separation of powers interact to protect our freedom.[9]

Not only are citizens ignorant, they are unaware and unconcerned about their ignorance. Most Americans spend more time engaged with game shows, reality television, technology, hobbies, sports, and entertainment gossip than on our political system. Critical thinking about our political issues and public affairs is rare. Although significant numbers of well-intentioned citizens are engaged in some manner in public policy, that participation is often ill-informed and shallow. Many are disillusioned – perhaps rightly so – about the role of public service and the political process. Like our politicians, much of the American public is blissfully unaware of the importance of our First Principles.

Americans are also disengaged. As one report explains, "Americans have turned away from politics and the public sphere in large numbers, leaving our civic life impoverished. Citizens are participating in public affairs less frequently, with less knowledge and enthusiasm, in fewer venues, and less equally than is healthy for a vibrant democratic polity."[10] Another study notes that "[t]here is an abundance of literature on the general decline of civic engagement among Americans."[11] Indeed, the "vast majority" of the leading "indicators of civic health show troubling declines over the last thirty years."[12] This disengagement has become particularly exacerbated and troubling in young adults[13] and high school dropouts.[14] The great bulk of Americans are unprepared to be responsible and active citizens.

This is not surprising given the abject performance of our schools in teaching American history and civics.[15] Only slightly more than a quarter of high school seniors are considered proficient in civics.[16] Stated another way, nearly 75% of high school seniors are incompetent to be citizens. As but one poignant example, only 5% of high school seniors can adequately explain checks on the President's power.[17] Over 70% of eighth graders are unable to explain the historical purpose of the Declaration of Independence, and more than half of high school seniors fail to satisfactorily describe the meaning of federalism.[18]

Only 13% of high school seniors are considered proficient in American history, and more than half are below the "basic" level.[19] Over 85% of high school students are unable to explain a reason for America's involvement in the Korean War, and 99% of eighth grade students are incapable of explaining how the fall of the Berlin Wall affected American foreign policy.[20] One of the members of the governing board of the National Assessment of Education Progress (NAEP) has acknowledged that the test results of high school students in American history are "abysmal."[21] Likewise, yet another study reveals that high school students possess fundamental misunderstandings of our free speech and press rights.[22] Most state standards for civic education are incomplete, poorly drafted, vague, unprioritized, and vacuous.[23] History standards fare no better.[24]

Over the last generation the amount of time high schools dedicate to civics and social studies has plummeted.[25] Meanwhile, a renewed emphasis on reading, math, and science has further pushed history and civics to the side-lines.[26] No wonder that a recent study by the National Conference for State Legislatures concluded that "young people do not understand the ideals of citizenship, they are disengaged from the political process, they lack the knowledge necessary for effective self-government, and their appreciation and support of American democracy is limited."[27]

By examining just one state – Michigan – we can begin to understand the crisis. Of the 106,866 high school students in the class of 2005 who took the social studies assessment test, 70,715 students (66%) failed to meet or exceed state standards; and 39,770 students (37%) were in the lowest category of assessment. Only 1331 students (1%) tested in the highest category of assessment. Meanwhile only 30% of eighth graders and 26% of fifth graders met or exceeded state standards. These are not simply statistics – they are our future leaders, clergy, judges, educators, soldiers, workers, managers, professors, volunteers, civil servants, firefighters, police, and voters. More shocking, of the 9,761 African American high school students who took the exam in 2001, 9,134 students failed to meet or exceed state standards, and eight – only eight – exceeded them.[28] Again, these are not simply statistics. These students are the future not only across the nation and Michigan, but most especially in the urban centers of Detroit, Lansing, Pontiac, and Flint. Michigan is not alone.[29]

The crisis does not stop in our fine institutions of higher learning. Nearly 80% of the seniors at fifty-five top colleges and universities, including Harvard and Princeton, received a D or F on a high school level American history test.[30] In fact, our colleges and universities generally "fail to increase knowledge about America's history and institutions."[31] Seniors at some Ivy League colleges actually know less than they did as freshmen; in other words, such institutions have a negative effect on historical knowledge.[32] Studies reveal that today's college graduates are no better prepared than high school graduates were fifty years ago.[33]

Our experiment in self-government, however, requires a vibrant understanding of our principles and engagement by an informed public. Most nations in world history were (and are) bound together by ethnicity, language, religion, custom, geography, or military might. Beginning anew, America was founded on a set of First Principles. Paraphrasing Abraham Lincoln, outgoing New York Mayor Rudolph Giuliani observed in his farewell address "that the test of your Americanism was not your family tree; the test of your Americanism was how much you believed in America. Because we're like a religion really. A secular religion. We believe in ideas and ideals."

Our political elite, media, educators, and public need to be well-informed about history, the First Principles, and the issues of the day to ensure that the republic functions effectively. Unlike a totalitarian dictatorship or authoritarian regime, our system is not intended to oppress, control, or exploit the people for the benefit of the governing elite. To the contrary, as Abraham Lincoln explained, ours is a republic of, by, and for the people; and a citizenry well-grounded in the basis of freedom is the only sure safeguard for protecting equality and unalienable rights. As Founding Father Dr Benjamin Rush observed, "Without learning, men become savages or barbarians, and where learning is confined to a *few* people, we always find monarchy, aristocracy, and slavery."[34]

Indeed, history is replete with free societies that failed because the people were unable or declined to vigorously defend their freedoms. The Weimar Republic elected Adolf Hitler to power. The Italian parliamentary democracy empowered Mussolini. The French Revolution, dedicated to liberty, equality, and fraternity, degenerated into the Terror and then Napoleon. The Russian democratic revolution morphed into seventy years of brutal Soviet Socialist totalitarianism. America has remained a free and just nation because its people and leaders historically had a deeply rooted understanding of their political rights and the gumption to defend them. So far, Americans have been able to resist the temptations of petty tyrants and utopians offered by an all powerful state. We would be fools to think that it must always remain so.

When they vote, our citizens should understand what they doing and why. When they participate in politics and agitate for change, our activists should be steeped in our historical traditions. When they fight and die for our country, our soldiers should do so out of a sense of the true greatness of our country – not from a visceral patriotic sense of duty as in Serbia, Chad, China, and Syria – but from deep knowledge and belief in the principles for which they fight. Our citizenry's ignorance jeopardizes our liberty; as our principles fade away in memory, so does our freedom.

Because we are not tending carefully to the fruits of liberty, they are beginning to rot. Today most Americans hold the government in very low esteem – and they do so because they are alienated, distrustful, and lack confidence in the very government that is intended to represent them.[35] Although one could argue that healthy skepticism about our government is exactly what we need, the skepticism is also a symptom and reflection of the public's sense, however vague, that our government is going askew. Just when an active citizenry is most needed, it has become disillusioned and disengaged. Huge government and trade deficits, political corruption, a poisonous political dialogue, an impending but all but ignored entitlement crisis, a tax code beyond comprehension, controversial foreign policy, the disgorgement of our manufacturing base, seemingly endless red tape and regulations, and an acute educational crisis that has lingered a generation are just some of the most obvious symptoms of the spoiling fruits of liberty.

We unconsciously rely on long-standing constitutional mechanisms to maintain our liberty. We have inherited the auxiliary precautions and critical features of the Constitution which preserve our freedom. By inertia and rote we still elect congressmen to pass laws; appoint our federal (and elect some state) judges to administer justice and review the law; and elect presidents to sign and veto legislation, conduct foreign affairs, and maintain civilian control over the military.

Yet because we have failed to provide consistent and vigorous maintenance of our system, the machine is breaking down. Many doubt whether the government really remains a republic accountable to the people. Many charge that the government is beholden to campaign donors, lobbyists, and special interest groups. Others assert that government policies directly undermine equality, religious freedom, property rights, and freedom from unreasonable search and seizure. Still others question whether the judiciary has been legislating from the bench – against the will of the people – in a quest to implement the judges' vision of enlightened social engineering. Many argue that the regulatory state is suffocating our liberty. Others posit that an imperial presidency is taking hold.

Whether any of these critiques is true is properly reserved for the subject of other works. In fact, each issue is extremely complex and could consume volumes of serious research and thoughtful debate. However, these issues can only be properly examined by those dedicated and insightful enough to review our history and First Principles – and apply those principles and history to current affairs. Instead, we have become enamored with sound-bites, appeals to our emotions, and superficial discussions regarding fundamental issues. Even while our nation is attacked by terrorists because of our exceptional nature, we ignore or denigrate our First Principles. We are losing our very ability to look to our founding history and principles to help us confront the critical challenges we face.

Some decry this alarm as foolish, since they believe that our First Principles are outdated and irrelevant to the challenges of the 21st century. To the contrary, understanding our First Principles is as critical today as when our republic was founded. At the dawn of the American Revolution, the political leaders who drafted and ratified the state constitutions replacing the old colonial governments often emphasized that "frequent recurrence to fundamental principles" was "necessary to preserve the blessings of liberty, and keep a government free."[36] Time has not eroded the truth of this maxim. The First Principles represent timeless truths that are of the utmost relevance for current policy problems and issues of the day.

Others, however, challenge the very legitimacy of the First Principles. Indeed, some leading academics, journalists, politicians, and social elites directly and indirectly attack our founding principles as irrelevant, backward, and false. Multiculturalists argue that our history is one of oppression and that our civilization is simply one of many equal alternatives. Equating America with military juntas, tribalism, fascism, and communist regimes is commonplace. Some claim, among other things, that the First Principles are Eurocentric, patriarchal, and exploitative. Many academics and social commentators vigorously attack America as unjust, with no discernable understanding of unalienable rights, the Social Compact, or the purpose and proper limit of government. Radio talk show hosts and columnists of all stripes eviscerate judges who simply follow the law as enacted by the legislature, as if the rule of law and republican government were insignificant. Politicians look to what is politically expedient, regardless of whether it supports or denigrates the First Principles.

This malaise is so ingrained in some sectors that on the first anniversary of the September 11 attacks, the National Education Association (NEA) adopted an extraordinarily disappointing approach to this indispensable teachable moment. The NEA's guidance to teachers on its website was to "create a low-key day of learning" and to plan "affirming activities – like planting memorial trees, doing murals or collages, writing poems or stories." The NEA advised parents to focus "on lessons learned – appreciating and getting along with people of diverse backgrounds and cultures, the importance of anger management and global awareness."

Although perhaps well-intentioned, this vapid counsel hardly did justice to one of the most horrific attacks on America in modern history. The authentic lessons learned – that there are Islamist extremists willing to kill themselves in order to slaughter thousands of innocent civilians because America is the earth's greatest hope for liberty and freedom – were simply ignored. The anniversary should be solemnly dedicated to reaffirming America's enduring principles – not trite and banal feel-good exercises.[37] The NEA's approach is symptomatic of a broader discomfort, if not downright loathing, of many educational leaders with promoting America's First Principles or a fair rendition of American history.

In fact, some educators have become stridently hostile to American civics and history. In a move so bold that Stalin, Hitler, and bin Laden could not even have dreamed of it, in 2006 the Michigan Department of Education's Social Studies Consultant and her supervisor announced that teachers should stop using the very words "America" and "American" in the classroom because: "It is ethnocentric for the United States to claim the entire hemisphere." Concerned that the sensibilities of Canadians, Mexicans, Cubans, and Brazilians would be offended, the Michigan Department of Education attempted to banish words that capture our very spirit. Fortunately, once this travesty was exposed in a guest commentary in *The Detroit News*, lambasted in the editorial pages, and extensively criticized on talk radio and elsewhere, the Department (after a few fits and starts) retreated.[38] However, the incident is but one blatant example of a strong undercurrent of anti-Americanism in education.

As the ill-advised attempts of the NEA and Michigan Department of Education illustrate, too many Americans take for granted the freedoms they enjoy while ignoring the dire need of our system to be reinvigorated and protected by those enjoying its blessings. The First Principles have transcended their original historical context and have been the engine of great social, political, and economic progress – resulting in phenomenal expansion of freedom and momentous improvement in racial, gender, social, and economic equality. As Part II will reveal, the unfulfilled promise of the First Principles is what motivated and drove America to eliminate slavery, enfranchise racial minorities and women, and strive for racial, social, and gender justice. Nearly universally ignored today is the critical maxim and warning that "The corruption of every government generally begins with that of its principles."[39] Those who ignore and denigrate our First Principles are aiding and abetting the corruption of America from within.

In addition to our domestic challenges, we face militant Islamist terrorists intent on destroying America. Like the USSR and Nazi Germany in the past, today's terrorists attack America because we are the living model of a free and just society.[40] In other words, the terrorists attack America because of the ideals by which we live and the foreign policy that reflects those ideals. Our struggle is most important, therefore, because of what we fight for. After all, any people – even one oppressed by a brutal dictatorship – will defend their nation when it is under attack from a foreign enemy. Unlike dozens of other armed conflicts around the world, defending the American dream makes our current struggle paramount to the future of just and free civilization. The terrorists will inevitably lose any shooting war, perhaps at great cost to our nation; but America will have suffered a greater loss if we slip into political amnesia. Put another way, what is the purpose of winning the war if we no longer care to remember the very ideals that provoked the attack of September 11?

Our greatest challenge is no longer a foreign nation or even terrorists armed with weapons of mass destruction, but preserving our liberty despite ourselves. The most powerful weapons against America are not guns and missiles, but ignorance, complacency, and disdain of our history and First Principles. America is dangerously close to allowing the flame of liberty to die out. We are patriotic, but have almost forgotten why. We are becoming puppet patriots – hollow and empty in meaning.[41]

Let there be no mistake. We may be fighting a hot war against militant Islamist terrorists today, but there is also a cold war raging, right here and right now, for the hearts and minds of our citizens – and we are losing. The terrorists have reminded us that some things are worth dying for. The rule of law, equality, empowering the people, unalienable rights, and limited government are such things. Our freedom was won with the blood and treasure of hundreds of thousands of our forebears. We must not allow their sacrifices to have been in vain. The crisis is here. We must dedicate ourselves to fanning the flame of liberty or risk it dying out. The terrorists, and all enemies of freedom, will win if we simply forget, or reject, what we are and the principles for which we stand. We cannot let those who hate America win by default. Simply put, we surrender when we abandon our First Principles. Political amnesia will be our death knell.

If we are to preserve our liberty and pass it on to posterity, we must rediscover and re-embrace our First Principles. The purpose of this work, therefore, is to reeducate our citizens about the First Principles so that we may fan the flame of liberty and reinvigorate the American dream for generations to come.

PART II
AMERICA'S FIRST PRINCIPLES AND FOUNDATIONAL HISTORY

We owe every other sacrifice to ourselves, to our federal brethren, and to the world at large, to pursue with temper and perseverance the great experiment which shall prove that man is capable of living in society, governing itself by laws, self-imposed, and securing to its members the enjoyment of life, liberty, property, and peace; and further to show, that even when government of its choice shall manifest a tendency to degeneracy, we are not at once to despair but that the will and the watchfulness of its sounder parts will reform its aberrations, recall it to original and legitimate principles, and restrain it within the rightful limits of self-government. Thomas Jefferson, *Draft Declaration and Protest of the Commonwealth of Virginia, on the Principles of the Constitution of the United States of America, and on the Violations of Them* (1825).

Part I of this book documents the crisis of ignorance and disdain America faces. Several complementary strategies to confront the crisis are detailed in Part III. However, to successfully implement those recommendations, we must understand our First Principles. We also must understand how they became the driving force of the American Revolution, the Constitution, and the civil rights movements – including the key figures and events that undertook such tremendous struggles. Unfortunately, the predominant textbooks and other major works fail to comprehensively, clearly, and fairly explain the First Principles and American history.[42] This part, therefore, provides such knowledge with the expectation that policy makers, media, educators, the legal profession, nonprofit organizations, and the general public will use it to follow and implement the recommendations outlined in Part III.

Chapter 2
America's First Principles

We hold these truths to be self-evident, that all men are created equal, that they are endowed by their Creator with certain unalienable rights, that among these are Life, Liberty, and the pursuit of Happiness. That to secure these rights, Governments are instituted among Men, deriving their just powers from the consent of the governed, That whenever any Form of Government becomes destructive of these ends, it is the Right of the People to alter or to abolish it, and to institute a new Government, laying its foundations on such principles and organizing its powers in such form, as to them shall seem likely to effect their Safety and Happiness. *Declaration of Independence of the United States of America* (1776).

❋ The *rule of law* is a First Principle that mandates that the law governs everyone

❋ The First Principle of *unalienable rights* recognizes that everyone is naturally endowed by their Creator with certain rights

❋ *Equality* is a First Principle that recognizes that all persons are created equal

❋ The First Principle of the *Social Compact* recognizes that governments are instituted by the people and derive their just powers from the consent of the governed

❋ The First Principle that the *protection of unalienable rights is the legitimate purpose and limit of government* requires the government to be strong enough to fulfill its purpose yet limited to that purpose

---

John Adams, Founding Father and second President of the United States, observed in 1776 that "We ought to consider what is the end of government, before we determine which is the best form."[43] Adams' prescription is peculiarly American. The United States of America, after all, was the first modern nation that founded its government on the basis of an end – the preservation of freedom.

America's First Principles arose from a revolutionary understanding of politics and government originating from English philosophers such as Thomas Hobbes, John Locke, John Milton, Algeron Sidney, and the Radical Whigs (the radical wing of the English parliamentary opposition during the 1700s).[44] The Founders' political philosophy holds that adherence to certain First Principles is a prerequisite to a free and just government. Each First Principle is an indispensable cornerstone of the American Republic; and each must be well-understood to secure our freedoms and continue the success of our grand experiment in self-government.

THE RULE OF LAW

For much of history, justifying the ruling government went no further than the point of a sword. As John Adams described, "In the earliest ages of the world, absolute monarchy seems to have been the universal form of government. Kings, and a few of their great counselors and captains, exercised a cruel tyranny over the people. . . ."[45] Thomas Jefferson, writing to Adams, added that with possible exception of the Dutch, "Either force or corruption has been the principle of every modern government. . . ."[46] Rulers mostly governed through fear – there were no citizens, only subjects beholden to the ruler. "When Louis XIV said, 'I am the state,' he expressed the essence of the doctrine of unlimited power," the great orator and politician Daniel Webster said. "By the rules of that system, the people are disconnected from the state; they are its subjects; it is their lord. These ideas, founded in the love of power, [were] long supported by the excess and abuse of it. . . ."[47]

Rulers often proffered some justification for their rule, such as divine right. However, as a practical matter, Pharaoh and King, Czar and Baron, and Daimyo and Emperor ruled by force. Such government still exists – Burma, Vietnam, Libya, North Korea, and Cuba are just a few examples where oppressive regimes continue to rule the people by the barrel of a gun. The Founding Fathers, however, believed that power is not justification, only explanation. Simply put, governments maintained by violence or the threat of violence are illegitimate and unjust. As Jefferson concisely observed, "force cannot give right."[48]

Even well-meaning rulers are likely to be corrupted when not required to obey the law. "Good laws make a good prince," observed Thomas Gordon, a leading English Radical Whig who was very influential in colonies, because even "the best men grow mischievous when they are set above laws. . . . There is something so wanton and monstrous in lawless power, that there scarce ever was a human spirit that could bear it. . . ."[49]

The Founders, therefore, understood as an "eternal truth" that the rule of law is a fundamental principle "upon which every free," honest, and legal "government must stand. . . ."[50] John Adams explained the Founders' understanding when he wrote that good government and the very definition of a republic "is an empire of laws."[51] Adams' distant cousin, Samuel Adams, noted that the "first principles of natural law and justice" include that the government "has no right to absolute arbitrary power over the lives and fortunes of the people . . . but it is bound to see that Justice is dispensed, and that the rights of the subjects be decided, by promulgated, standing and known laws. . . ."[52]

Setting aside the tyranny of the past, George Washington could accurately remark that the American system "is purely, a government of Laws made and executed by the fair substitutes of the people alone."[53] In America, the government is to govern the citizenry according to the law, not by the whims or fancies of the men and women who happen to hold positions of power at any given moment. By requiring our political leaders to enact and publish the law, and to adhere to the same law that applies to each citizen, the rule of law acts as a strong barrier against tyrannical and arbitrary government.[54]

One potent example of the nation's adherence to the rule of law was the unprecedented resignation of President Richard Nixon in 1974. Proving that even the most powerful man in the world is not above the law, constitutional processes forced Nixon to resign when his re-election campaign's burglary of the Democratic National Committee's headquarters at the Watergate and his attempts to cover up the crime were exposed. Vice President Gerald Ford was sworn in as the President. Ford assured the country at his swearing-in ceremony that Nixon's resignation and his assumption of power was an affirmation of the rule of law. "My fellow Americans, our long national nightmare is over," Ford eloquently observed. "Our Constitution works. Our great Republic is a government of laws and not of men."[55] Nothing proved Ford's words more true than Nixon's resignation and Ford's seamless assumption of power.

The rule of law also requires that the same law govern all citizens. Samuel Adams observed that the rule of law means that "There shall be one rule of Justice for the rich and the poor; for the favorite in Court, and the Countryman at the Plough."[56] United States Supreme Court Justice John Marshall Harlan similarly reflected that "in view of the constitution, in the eye of the law, there is in this country no superior, dominant, ruling class of citizens. There is no caste here. . . . In respect of civil rights, all citizens are equal before the law. The humblest is the peer to the most powerful."[57]

That our citizens must abide by the law is essential to the rule of law. In his *Farewell Address* (1796), Washington observed that "The very idea of the power and right of the People to establish Government presupposes the duty of every Individual to obey the established Government. All obstructions to the execution of the Laws . . . are destructive of this fundamental principle and of fatal tendency." Abraham Lincoln reaffirmed Washington's view by recognizing that the failure of our citizens to adhere to the law would lead to chaos and anarchy. In his famous *Speech Before the Young Men's Lyceum of Springfield, Illinois* (1838), Lincoln pleaded: "Let every American, every lover of liberty, every well-wisher to his posterity swear by the blood of the Revolution never to violate in the least particular the laws of the country, and never to tolerate their violation by others." He explained that adherence to the rule of law, even in the face of unpopular or unjust laws, was critical to preserving freedom and liberty:

> As the patriots of seventy-six did to the support of the
> Constitution and the laws let every American pledge his life,
> his property, and his sacred honor. Let every many remem-
> ber that to violate the law is to trample on the blood of his
> father, and to tear the charter of his own and his children's
> liberty. . . . And, in short, let it become the political religion
> of the nation; and let the old and the young, the rich and the
> poor, the grave and the gay of all sexes and tongues and col-
> ors and conditions, sacrifice unceasingly upon its altars. . . .

When I so pressingly urge a strict observance of all the laws, let me not be understood as saying there are no bad laws, or that grievances may not arise for the redress of which no legal provisions have been made. I mean to say no such thing. But I do mean to say that although bad laws, if they exist, should be repealed as soon as possible, still, while they continue in force, for the sake of example they should be religiously observed.

Echoing Lincoln's remarks nearly 130 years later, President John F. Kennedy insightfully observed that "Our nation is founded on the principle that observance of the law is the eternal safeguard of liberty and defiance of the law is the surest road to tyranny."[58]

By requiring our leaders and citizens to be governed by the same law, the rule of law is the foundation of all of our liberties. The Constitution and the law, after all, would be irrelevant if they did not authentically govern our political leadership and citizenry. As Dr Joseph Warren, a leading colonial figure of the movement toward the Revolution, remarked, "If charters are not deemed sacred, how miserably precarious is everything founded on them."[59] Nothing is more common in modern history than a government that crushed the freedom of its citizens despite a piece of paper, labeled a constitution, purportedly prohibiting the government's oppressive actions.

The entire American constitutional order designed to secure our freedom presupposes the rule of law. Washington explained in his *Farewell Address* that "Respect for [the Constitution's] authority, compliance with its Laws, acquiescence in its measures, are duties enjoined by the fundamental maxims of true Liberty." Due process, freedom of speech, freedom of religion, freedom from arbitrary arrest and searches, the right to vote, and all other individual rights are animated by the rule of law and lifeless without it. Structural protections such as the separation of powers and checks and balances are vacuous "parchment barriers" without a vigorous dedication to their enforcement.[60] Without an underlying commitment to the rule of law, courts do not dispense justice because their decisions are not based in the law, but on personal preferences; the legislature does not enact the will of the people, but its own whims; and the executive does not enforce the law but its own desires. Accordingly, that we shall have "a government of laws and not of men" is the bedrock of the First Principles.[61]

UNALIENABLE RIGHTS

The *Declaration of Independence* proclaims that another First Principle is a self-evident truth: "all men are endowed, by their Creator, with certain unalienable rights; that among these are life, liberty, and the pursuit of happiness." This precept was nurtured in the Founding Fathers by John Locke and other English natural law philosophers. Jefferson explained the essence of the Founders' understanding regarding this First Principle: "a free people claims their rights as derived from the laws of nature, and not as a gift from their chief magistrate."[62] That this principle forms much of the philosophical bulwark of our founding is evidenced by its recognition not only in the *Declaration of Independence*, but in the state constitutions adopted during and in the aftermath of the Revolution.[63] Thus, a basic maxim of American government is the recognition that some rights derived from Nature may not be taken or violated by the government.

This First Principle and its sources turned topsy-turvy the prior understanding of authority and rights. Putting aside a few ancient democracies and republics, Kings and nobility historically were the origin of authority (*i.e.*, the sovereign), and they granted rights and privileges to their subjects. The privileged class was the sole power and authority, and the people held their liberties at the pleasure of the rulers. Even in England, perhaps the most enlightened country at the time of the Revolution, the King was considered supreme. While the House of Commons was, in a limited sense, intended to recognize the rights of the people, it was only one of three branches of government, and both the monarchy and the House of Lords possessed enormous authority that was derived from blood and heritage.

Although the Radical Whigs and a smattering of English parliamentarians embraced the concept that the people were (or should be) sovereign, nearly no one supported abolishing the monarchy and the House of Lords (and both exist even today). The political reality in England and across the globe at the time of the Revolution – and for most of the world throughout history

– was that the people were not the sovereign, but the ruled. This is why residents of the British Empire were not referred to as citizens, but subjects.[64]

Nevertheless, America boldly proclaimed at its birth that some rights were endowed by man's very nature – and that individuals are incapable of relinquishing them. Because these rights are endowed in people from Nature's God, they are inherent in each individual and cannot be abandoned – in other words, such rights are unalienable. These unalienable rights are so important and intrinsic to humanity that no person can forfeit them by simply consenting to live under the rule of a government.[65] John Dickinson – an early American colonial opponent of tyrannical British actions – powerfully expressed this understanding in 1766:

> We claim [rights essential to happiness] from a higher source
> – from the King of kings, and Lord of all the earth. They
> are not annexed to us by parchments and seals. They are
> created in us by the decrees of Providence, which establish
> the laws of our nature. They are born with us; exist with us;
> and cannot be taken from us by any human power without
> taking our lives. In short, they are founded on the immu-
> table maxims of reason and justice.[66]

John Adams likewise explained that the people possessed rights that were "undoubtedly, antecedent to all earthly government – *Rights*, that cannot be repealed or restrained by human laws – *Rights*, derived from the great Legislator of the universe."[67] Like many other state constitutions adopted during and after the Revolution, the Virginia Bill of Rights, drafted by the influential revolutionary leader George Mason (and adopted just prior to the *Declaration of Independence*), proclaimed that all men "by nature . . . have certain inalienable rights, of which, when they enter into a state of society, they cannot, by any compact, deprive their posterity; namely, the enjoyment of life and liberty, with the means of acquiring and possessing property, and pursuing and obtaining happiness and safety."[68]

In other words, "the sacred rights of mankind," Alexander Hamilton observed, "are not to be rummaged for among old parchments or musty records. They are written, as with a sunbeam, in the whole *volume* of human nature, by the hand of divinity itself, and can never be erased or obscured by mortal power."[69] Thus, the recognition and protection of unalienable rights is a centerpiece of America's First Principles.

EQUALITY

The Founding Fathers based a further First Principle upon another self-evident truth recognized in the *Declaration of Independence* – that "all men are created equal." The Founders embraced the Judeo-Christian understanding of the Creator – an understanding that the Creator created all individuals, that each person arises from His handiwork, and that every person embodies His blessing.

Regardless of physical and mental differences between individuals, and despite disparities in wealth or station, each individual, as His creation, is equally precious in His eyes. Each person has dignity before God; and no person is elevated above his fellow man. Most important, each is loved equally by the Creator, and each is judged by his or her deeds and intentions. Thus, putting aside the theological briar patch of predestination, each has an equal opportunity to obtain redemption from sin or damnation, and each chooses his or her own path.

While this First Principle originally arose from a belief in the nature of the Creator, the laws of nature lead many to the same conclusion. Undoubtedly, human evolution and nature have created subtle (or sometimes, not so subtle) differences in each person, yet nature itself grants each individual the right to pursue his or her needs and desires. To compete in a state of nature, each person possesses the same opportunity – the same right embedded in his or her very nature – to maintain his or her survival and to pursue happiness.

If the beasts of nature are equally free to engage in the struggle for survival without Nature's God imposing capricious restrictions on their actions, then men are entitled to no less. More precisely, in a state of nature, all individuals are equal not because of their capabilities (in which case all persons are unequal, having different capabilities), but because they are entitled to at least plan, desire, and attempt to undertake the same actions as all others. Inevitably the results will differ, but the ability to pursue like goals are not denied by nature. Likewise, the state of nature dictates that all persons are entitled to nurture their families, to establish and defend a home, secure their liberty from attack from nature or other persons, and to pursue happiness.[70]

By embracing the First Principle of equality, the Founding Fathers once again rejected the deliberately inequitable regimes dominating the globe in their time. Inequality codified in the law was a cornerstone of government throughout world history. Hereditary nobility and other special classes were almost universally granted special privileges unknown to the common person.

Even in England, the modern birthplace of the rule of law, the law continued to bolster and elevate the nobility. Likewise, in 1776 the French were over a decade away from overthrowing a regime that divided the society into three estates, with the first and second estates (the nobility and clergy) possessing oppressive powers embodied in the law. The caste system defined India; similar divisions were inherent in the other great powers.

Modern history is also replete with such societies. South Africa during apartheid segregated its society by race; the Soviet Union divided its society among classes, ethnic groups, creed, and party; and Nazi Germany committed genocide in the pursuit of Aryan superiority. Whether based on class, caste, religion, race, tribe, ethnic group, economic status, language, party membership, eugenics, or otherwise, governments throughout most of world history have maintained divisions among individuals and groups of individuals. These divisions were often woven into the fundamental law of the society. Such governments were based on the proposition of the inherent inequality of all people.

From its very founding, however, America aspired to embody the First Principle that all men are created equal. Not only did the *Declaration of Independence* affirm this principle, so did the state constitutions that were drafted and ratified following the *Declaration of Independence*. Those constitutions consistently state in some form "That all men are by nature equally free and independent."[71] In 1863 Abraham Lincoln reaffirmed this founding principle in the *Gettysburg Address* when he explained that the nation was "conceived in liberty and dedicated to the proposition that all men are created equal."

This equality of each individual, however, is one of rights and opportunity – not results. In other words, as the Fourteenth Amendment states, each individual is entitled to "equal protection of the laws." This equal protection, however, does not require that the government attempt to equalize the social status, wealth, and property of individuals. Equality before the law simply requires that each individual, irrespective of race, color, creed, nationality, wealth, social status, religion, and similar characteristics, be treated equally by the government. Wealthy white Lutheran men, therefore, should be subject to the same treatment under the law as poor Muslim women, and vice versa. Combined with the rule of law, this First Principle requires that each person be treated equally under the law, and that the equal protection of the laws be afforded to all.

THE SOCIAL COMPACT

The *Declaration of Independence* also recognizes another First Principle as a self-evident truth: "governments are instituted among men, deriving their just powers from the consent of the governed. . . ." There are two aspects to this First Principle. The first holds that legitimate governments are instituted among the people; the second that the just powers of the government are derived from the consent of the people. Like the other First Principles, the Founders derived much of their understanding of this First Principle from John Locke and other like-minded philosophers.

Locke and the Founders not only believed that all individuals are vested with unalienable rights, they also believed that most rights are not absolute. They understood that the right to grow wheat does not permit one to steal another's bread. In a state of nature, each person was free to pursue his or her own interests – food, shelter, love, family, material goods – without regard to established rules of conduct. In Utopia, each person would exercise those rights granted by Nature without interfering with the rights of others. However, Utopia is St Thomas More's fantasy, and conflict is inevitable without established laws and norms of conduct. Cain possessed the right to farm and make offerings to God, but his jealousy did not grant him the right to slay Abel. As the story of Cain and Abel reveals, conflict arises from man's very nature. After all, there appears to be an infinite number of causes for strife – greed, fear, hate, love, pride, vainglory, competition, desire, lust, religion, resources, power, evil, mental illness, addiction, and jealously being just some of the more obvious examples.

Of course, as Locke observed, a person unjustly assaulted by another may, by the "fundamental law of nature," protect himself, his family, and his property.[72] The result: war. The English philosopher Thomas Hobbes explained in his treatise, *Leviathan*:

> Out of civil states, there is always war of every one against every one. Hereby it is manifest, that during the time men live without a common power to keep them all in awe, they are in that condition which is called war; and such a war, as is of every man, against every man. . . .

> In such condition, there is no place for industry; because the fruit thereof is uncertain: and consequently no culture of the earth; no navigation, or use of the commodities that may be imported by sea; no commodious building; no instruments of moving and removing, such things as require much force; no knowledge of the face of the earth; no account of time; no arts; no letters; no society; and which is worst of all; continual fear and danger of violent death; and the life of man, solitary, poor, nasty, brutish, and short.[73]

Locke, Hobbes, and the Founders posited that to escape such war, individuals united in civil societies and established government to secure the peace by delegating their individual authority to the collective. Locke noted that there could be "no freedom" without a Social Compact of laws, because "liberty is to be free from restraint and violence from others; which cannot be where there is no law."[74] James Madison reflected that "If men were angels, no government would be necessary."[75] But men are not angels, Hamilton noted, and government becomes necessary to restrain "the passions of men."[76]

Thus, paradoxically, legal restraints are necessary to preserve liberty. By relinquishing certain rights of nature, an individual gains overall security. Without each individual's relinquishment of some of his or her natural rights to society, chaos reigns. To secure one's life, liberty, and property, one has no choice but to unite in a civil society that will defend those rights in exchange for the relinquishment of others. By "entering into the social compact, though the individual parts with a portion of his natural rights," James Wilson, a leading

Founding Father explained before the Pennsylvania Ratifying Convention, "it is evident that he gains more by the limitation of the liberty of others, than he loses by the limitation of his own, – so that in truth, the aggregate of liberty is more in society, than it is in a state of nature."[77]

Individuals, therefore, relinquish the right to judge and punish others for wrongdoing and delegate that authority to law enforcement and the justice system. The alternative is vigilantism with all of its accompanying Hobbesian horrors. Similarly, individuals relinquish the right to create their own rules of conduct by delegating that authority to legislators, so that a universal system of laws may provide uniformity, certainty, and consensus in daily life.

The American experiment was founded on this understanding of the Social Compact. The sentiments of Wilson, Madison, Hamilton, and others attending the Constitutional Convention were often echoed in the Revolutionary era. The Massachusetts Constitution, for example, recognized that "The body politic is formed by a voluntary association of individuals: it is a social compact, by which the whole people covenants with each citizen, and each citizen with the whole people, that all shall be governed by certain laws for the common good."[78] That this was a widely held sentiment is confirmed by a passage written by the Constitutional Convention in the letter accompanying the newly drafted Constitution to Congress (1787): "Individuals entering into society, must give up a share of liberty to preserve the rest."

This understanding that individuals establish the government to protect their rights leads to the second aspect of the Social Compact – that the people form the basis of the government and must consent to give the government its authority. Robert Bates, a delegate to the Constitutional Convention, explained that "In every free government, the people must give their assent to the laws by which they are governed. This is the true criterion between a free government and an arbitrary one." In reality, no government directly asks each individual to consent to its governance or to approve each exercise of governmental authority. However, in America citizens are free to emigrate or stay; individuals pay taxes which are voted upon by the people; individuals freely take advantage of the security and benefits offered by the state; and the government derives its authority directly from the vote of its people. America clearly embodies the First Principle of the Social Compact.

Perhaps a few ancient cities and short-lived republics justified their governments through the consent of the people, but in the modern age at least, none explicitly embraced the principle until the establishment of the United States. As James Wilson explained as a delegate before the Constitutional Convention, the Founding Fathers believed that "all authority was derived from the people." Thomas Paine, a leading American revolutionary, agreed that a government founded upon the consent of the people "is the only mode in which Governments have a right to arise, and the only principle on which they have a right to exist."[79] No wonder then that the Revolutionary-era state constitutions declared that "government of right originates from the people, is founded in consent, and instituted for the general good."[80] Indeed, the American Revolution was strongly motivated by a defense of this First Principle. The cry of "no taxation without representation" was directly derived from this principle. The Social Compact is an indispensable First Principle.

SECURING RIGHTS: THE PURPOSE AND LIMIT OF GOVERNMENT

The First Principle of the Social Compact generates two logical possibilities regarding the scope and reach of governmental authority: either (i) the sovereign, to preserve the peace and maintain order, is all powerful, or (ii) the sovereign, because it has been granted its power to preserve the unalienable rights of individuals, is limited to possessing only those powers necessary to the accomplish that aim. The choice, at its extreme, becomes absolute power or a limited, free government.

Hobbes' vision was clear: absolute power. According to Hobbes, because individuals have consented to be ruled by the government, the government can do no wrong. Hence, no limits upon governmental power are necessary. Doctrines such as limited government, federalism, and respect for individual rights are unnecessary because the will of the people reigns supreme over individual rights and desires. Hobbes asserted that "Nothing done to a man by his own consent can be injury."[81] Hobbes' conception of consent simply required an individual to consent to being a member of the society. Thus, an individual need not consent to particular governmental powers or specific acts; he or she simply submitted to the rule of the government for all purposes. In short, Hobbes advocated the view that the sovereign has control over all things, including life, liberty, property, and justice.

In essence, Hobbes justified the later tyranny of the Soviet Empire and Mao's communist China – both were supposedly based on the unfettered power of the people. Fascist Italy also subscribed to the principles that the sovereign – *i.e.*, the corporate state – possessed unchecked power. In totalitarian regimes, the authority of the government overrides the rights of all of its subjects.

Hobbes justifies oppression even in republics. While *Leviathan* was written to defend the power of the English monarchy, its premise also supports unfettered democratic regimes. After all, in a republic the majority of the people elect their lawmakers. So vested with the consent of the governed, Hobbes' doctrine would provide that a representative government can do no wrong and has unlimited power. Yet, a representative government is just as capable as a dictatorship in oppressing individual rights. Hitler was elected Fuhrer through the suicide of a popularly-elected assembly.

Perhaps more instructive was the elected National Convention of the French Revolution. Replacing the unfettered power of the King with the unfettered power of the nation, no laws, constitutional barriers, or unalienable rights would stand in the way of the will of the people. Emmanuel Joseph Sieyès, an early philosophical leader of the French Revolution, explained that "it is sufficient for [the nation's] will to be manifested for all positive law to vanish before it. In whatever form the nation wills, it is sufficient that it does will: all forms are good, and its will is always the supreme law." Hence, the Declaration of Rights of 1793 specifically provided that "any individual who usurps the sovereignty of the people shall be instantly put to death by free men." No wonder then that a commission established by members of the Committee of Public Safety could state in its Instruction of November 16, 1793 that "A revolutionary agent may do anything." The rule of law degenerated completely into the boundless rule of the majority. The National Assembly massacred tens of thousands, commissioned the guillotine against its own members, and devoured heroes of the revolution as quickly as they were anointed – all in the name of the will of the people.

The Founding Fathers rejected the doctrine of Hobbes and adopted its opposite as a First Principle – that the powers of the government are limited to those necessary to protect the unalienable rights of the people and necessary auxiliary authority. This First Principle was recognized by the *Declaration of*

Independence when it provided that "to secure these rights . . . governments are instituted among men. . . ." After all, "it is," Jefferson explained, "to secure our just rights that we resort to government at all. . . ."[82]

Paine expressed the American sentiment when he wrote that "Man did not enter into society to become *worse* than he was before, not to have fewer rights than he had before, but to have those rights better secured."[83] Thus, in America, Jefferson explained, "our rulers can have authority over such natural rights only as we have submitted to them."[84] Because individuals relinquished some of their rights solely to secure their liberty and property, Locke wrote, the government "can have no other end or measure when in the hands of the magistrates but to preserve the members of that society in their lives, liberties, and possessions; and so cannot be an absolute, arbitrary power over their lives and fortunes which are so much as possible to be preserved. . . ." In other words, the government "can never have a right to destroy, enslave, or designedly to impoverish the subjects."[85]

Although government is necessary, it is not something to be relished and encouraged. To the contrary, the Founders believed that government should be strictly limited to its proper purposes. Thomas Paine's *Common Sense* (1776) may have best captured the particular American sentiment of robust skepticism regarding the role of the government in the Social Compact:

> [G]overnment even in its best state is but a necessary evil; in its worst state an intolerable one . . . Government, like dress, is the badge of lost innocence; the palaces of the kings are built on the ruins of the bowers of paradise. For were the impulses of conscience clear, uniform, and irresistibly obeyed, man would need no other lawgiver; but that not being the case, he finds it necessary to surrender up a part of his property to furnish means for the protection of the rest. . . . Here then is the origin and rise of government; namely, a mode rendered necessary by the inability of moral virtue to govern the world; here too is the design and end of government, *viz.* freedom and security.

Put another way, because the authority of the government is derived from individuals, it possesses no power beyond the just authority of a single individual in a state of nature. Thus, directly opposed to the proposition that the collective society is all powerful, a just government has only the authority individuals relinquished to it. As Jefferson wrote, "the rights of the whole can be no more than the sum of the rights of individuals."[86] "For being but the joint power of every member of the society given up to that person, or assembly, which is legislator," Locke explained, "it can be no more than those persons had in a state of nature before they entered into society, and gave it up to the community." In short, we have consented to the government to protect our unalienable rights, and, therefore, have only granted it such power as it needs to perform that function and auxiliary supports thereof, nothing more. From its founding, America embraced as a First Principle that the purpose and limit of the government is protecting the unalienable rights of its citizens.

THE FOUNDATION OF A FREE AND JUST GOVERNMENT

Alexander Hamilton powerfully explained the critical need to adhere to our First Principles: "A government which does not rest on the laws of justice, rests on that of force. There is no middle ground."[87] The rule of law; the recognition and protection of unalienable rights; equality; the Social Compact; and securing rights as the purpose and limit of government – these are the First Principles that our Founders embraced. This is the high ground that must be defended to secure our freedom.

As the remainder of Part II of this work reveals, our Founders heeded Hamilton's warning. When these First Principles were violated by the British Crown, the Founders invoked the final First Principle – the right to rebel against an oppressive government. After all, the Declaration of Independence also recognized that "it is the right of the people to alter or abolish" a government that is oppressive to the ends of the other First Principles, and that the people have the right "to institute a new Government, laying its foundation on such principles, and organizing its powers in such form, as to them shall seem most likely to effect their Safety and Happiness." Following the Revolution, the Founders incorporated the First Principles into the Constitution and the life of the body politic, thereby setting the foundation by which America was to be free and establish a just government.

Chapter 3
Liberty in the Wilderness

Our fathers having nobly resolved never to wear the yoke of despotism, and seeing the European world, at the time, through indolence and cowardice, falling a prey to tyranny, bravely threw themselves upon the bosom of the ocean, determined to find a place in which they might enjoy their freedom, or perish in the glorious attempt. Approving heaven beheld the favourite ark dancing upon the waves, and graciously preserved it until the chosen families were brought in safety to these western regions. Dr Joseph Warren, *Second Oration Commemorating the Boston Massacre* (1775).

---

* The American colonies were an asylum for settlers from Europe who were fleeing religious and other persecution; others came with the hope of obtaining a better life

* The colonies embodied the Social Compact – new governments and societies were created from a clean slate

* The colonists possessed the unalienable rights of Englishmen and began to recognize other liberties

* The colonists were generally allowed to exercise self-government

* Equality was a social reality in the colonies

The New World presented immigrating Europeans a novel opportunity to begin anew. Eager to escape the cruelties of Europe or to find riches, they chose to settle in America (either as freemen or indentured servants) and establish societies in the wilderness. The theory of the Social Compact came to life in America. While Locke and Hobbes had only theorized about the origins of primordial societies, America became a living experiment of societies created through a compact of the governed.[88]

The Puritans are perhaps the best-known example. "Puritanism was not merely a religious doctrine," Alexis de Tocqueville observed, "but it corresponded in many points with the most absolute democratic and republican theories. . . . Puritanism . . . was scarcely less a political than a religious doctrine. No sooner had the emigrants landed on the barren coast . . . than it was their care to constitute a society."[89] The Puritans did so by subscribing to the Mayflower Compact in 1620. Perhaps for the first time in history, the Mayflower Compact placed into practice Locke's theory of the Social Compact by establishing a community government by a written agreement signed by the governed. The Mayflower Compact provided as follows:

> IN THE NAME OF GOD, AMEN. We, whose names are underwritten. . . . Do by these presents, solemnly and mutually in the Presence of God and one another, covenant and combine, ourselves together into a civil body politick, for our better ordering and preservation, and furtherance of the ends aforesaid: and by virtue hereof do enact, constitute, and frame such just and equal laws, ordinances, acts, constitutions, and offices, from time to time, as shall be thought most meet and convenient for the general good of the Colony: unto which we promise all due submission and obedience. *The First Charter of Massachusetts* (1629).

Other colonies also established havens of freedom based on a Social Compact. While some came to America to escape oppressive poverty, to win fortunes, or were brought here in manacles, most, as the Second Continental Congress explained, "left their native land, to seek on these shores a residence for civil and religious freedom."[90] The recognition and protection of unalienable rights as the purpose of government, therefore, took early and deep root in America.

The Puritans, for example, fled to America to escape religious persecution in England. Native son of Massachusetts John Adams explained that it was the "love of universal liberty, and a hatred, a dread, a horror, of the infernal" British government that "accomplished the settlement of America."[91] Adams was drawing upon his experience in Massachusetts, the safe harbor for Puritans. In fact, like many of the Founding Fathers, Adams came to exemplify what common men could accomplish in a land of freedom. The son of a modest preacher, Adams became a school teacher, renowned lawyer, leading revolutionary, Vice President, and second President of the United States. While in Europe, on his own initiative he secured loans from the Dutch that funded – really saved – the Revolution. "Every member of Congress in 1776 acknowledged him to be the first man in the House. Dr Brownson (of Georgia) used to say that when he spoke, he fancied an angel was let down from heaven to illuminate the Congress."[92] His was the will that compelled Congress to adopt the *Declaration of Independence*.

Like Adams, many colonists fulfilled their dreams and aspirations. While some colonies focused upon profits – Virginians, for example, feverishly began to plant cash crops such as tobacco – other colonies became sanctuaries for the persecuted. Massachusetts, Pennsylvania, and Maryland were established to protect minority religious sects from oppression.

Moreover, the colonists planted their new governments in the rich soil of English conceptions of liberty. Although religious dissenters and others fled the persecution of England, Great Britain was paradoxically peculiar in this age for the protection of freedom. Like the other great European powers of the eighteenth century, Great Britain was ruled by a hereditary monarch. Yet, unlike the strongest of the continental powers, the British King was not absolute. The King shared power with Parliament – a legislative assembly composed of a hereditary House of Lords and an elected House of Commons.

Moreover, the power of Kings was limited by powerful feudal lords. Throughout English history, Kings, Commons, and Lords clashed – often with catastrophic results for all parties – and the nation. However, out of these clashes came the recognition of certain rights and principles of liberty that had become fundamental to the governance of the British Empire at the time of the American Revolution – due process of law; the legitimacy of the Commons as representatives of the non-noble people; taxation requiring the approval of the Commons; a relatively free press; the sovereignty of the people; and the rule of law (*i.e.*, that all members of society, including King and Parliament, were bound by the law). On the other hand, the legitimacy of the King's rule was unquestioned; the nobility firmly entrenched; the Church of England strictly controlled religious affairs and persecuted dissenters; and the sovereignty of the people, while invoked, was hardly a political reality.

The American colonies, however, possessed a unique perspective regarding English rule – they were not only nurtured in the soil of English rights and liberty, but they were also nearly immune to the corrupting influence of King and Parliament. Disinterested in the fringes of the empire, Great Britain was unwilling to invest much in the initial establishment of the colonies. Benjamin Franklin could rightly observe with only a little exaggeration that the colonies were "acquired, purchased, or conquered, at the sole expense of the settlers, or their ancestors; without the aid of the mother country."[93]

Indeed, "The crown of England looked with indifference" upon the colonies.[94] Thousands of miles from the heart of the Empire and established and maintained with little imperial support, the colonists were free to govern their domestic affairs. Edmund Burke, the English member of Parliament and brilliant political philosopher who sympathized with America during the Revolutionary era, dubbed the prevailing British policy toward the American colonies as "salutary neglect." There were no bishops stationed in America, no hereditary aristocracy, and no significant interference with the daily lives of the colonists. While colonists enjoyed the protection of the English fleet, and on occasion the army, they were not dominated by those forces.

Even the royal governors appointed by the crown possessed little authentic power. Each colony had established an elected representative assembly composed of colonists. These assemblies, like the Parliament in Britain, controlled each colony's treasury and slowly chipped away at their governors' authority and autonomy. The first assembly, established by Sir Edwin Sandys (an opposition member of Parliament) was founded in Virginia in 1619 to oppose a corrupt and rather cruel governor. This perception of the righteous role of the legislative assembly persisted throughout the colonial period.

Moreover, many colonists came to America from continental Europe, outside of the British Empire, and, therefore, had no allegiance to the British Empire. Some, like the Irish, even possessed an intense hatred toward

England. Others, such as the Quakers and Puritans, emigrated to America to escape British oppression. As one foreign observer noted, "Here individuals of all nations are melted into a new race of men, whose labors and posterity will one day cause great changes in the world."[95] Most colonists, therefore, had no enduring love of the crown. With the exception of royal governors and the small influence they gained from the minimal patronage they bestowed, there was little binding the colonists to the crown and empire other than tradition, respect, and loyalty. Although English rule and allegiance to the crown in the colonies were shallow, there was no compelling reason to upset it. In fact, the colonists prospered under their relative autonomy, and the empire's military assistance would on occasion recall the need for her protection.

The most notable exception to the policy of salutary neglect was the imposition of the system of mercantilism on American commerce. Through the Navigation Acts, England generally required Americans to trade solely with the mother country. The policy usually amounted to Americans exporting less expensive raw goods and importing more expensive finished products. Nevertheless, Americans' adeptness at smuggling lessened the burden of even that influence. In any event, many Americans enjoyed substantial benefits under the mercantile system; when not, many simply evaded it.

Americans enjoyed freedom not only from the crown, but from governmental authority in general. For the most part, the colonial representative assemblies did not interfere with the daily life of the colonists. Taxation was light. Those rights protected in England were also protected in America, and other rights, such as the right to be free from religious persecution and an established church, were beginning to be recognized in the colonies for the first time in the modern world. Maryland protected Catholics; Pennsylvania shielded Quakers; and Rhode Island was a sanctuary for many.

Free of oppressive taxes and tyrannical governmental policies that had driven them into poverty overseas, men were free to make a living. Due to the abundance of inexpensive land, most freemen were self-sufficient and independent landowners. This in turn produced an equality of opportunity and condition unparalleled to that point in history. With no landed hereditary nobility, each family was free to take hold of every economic opportunity in their own fashion. For the most part, men were self-made, without the help or hindrance of King or Parliament.

Dr Joseph Warren expressed the prevailing sentiment when he stated that "The colonist found himself free, and thought himself secure; he dwelt under his own vine, and under his own fig tree, and had none to make him afraid. . . ."[96] The standard of living, while often austere in comparison to the higher European classes, was quite good compared to the lower European classes. Moreover, the colonists' standard of living was rising. The Southern colonies began to prosper as they became commercial and trading outposts in the New World. Immigrants from other European nations, as well as slaves who were excluded from the Social Compact, began to arrive *en masse*. The relative good health of Americans was witnessed by their rapidly growing population that doubled every twenty years.

J. Hector St John de Crèvecoeur, who came to America during the French and Indian War, observed the formation of the American spirit:

> In this great American asylum, the poor of Europe have by some means met together. . . . Urged by a variety of motives, here they came. Everything has tended to regenerate them: new laws, a new mode of living, a new social system; here they become men: In Europe they were as so many useless plants, wanting vegetative mould and refreshing showers; they withered, and were mowed down by want, hunger, and war; but now, by the power of transplantation, like other plants they have token root and flourished! Formerly they were not numbered in any civil lists of their country, except in those of the poor; here they rank as citizens.[97]

Also vitally important, as a nation of freeholders, equality was not an abstraction, but a reality. Colonists clearly embraced the core idea of equality – that all men are equal before the law and equally endowed with unalienable rights. This belief had practical effects in the very creation of the Social Compact – only equal men could enter into the compact. This belief, however, had a more permanent effect since equality in the social sphere produced equality in the political arena. Nearly all freeholders (*i.e.,* property holders) could vote, and since nearly all white men were freeholders, nearly all freemen held the franchise. While patronage dominated governance, almost any freeman could rise beyond his humble beginnings and participate in politics.

Indeed, many of the Founding Fathers rose from rather humble backgrounds in their own or their parents' generation. Benjamin Franklin, for instance, was born in Boston to a modest family and apprenticed by his brother (against his will) as a printer. He soon engaged in politics, clerked for the Pennsylvania Legislature, and served as a member of that body. In turn, he served as a colonial agent in London, a member of the First Continental Congress, Minister to France, and a leading delegate to the Constitutional Convention. Personifying the various talents of Americans, he also had time to develop innovative printing techniques, publish almanacs, invent the Franklin stove, and discover electricity.

Of course, entire segments of society, such as slaves, Native Americans, and women, were ill-served by colonial society and excluded from the body politic; but for those recognized in the colonial polity, America was truly the land of the free. Like Franklin, Americans controlled their political and economic destinies and expected to continue to do so indefinitely. Through enormous personal sacrifice and daily struggle, they tamed the wilderness and established a proud society. They embraced the rule of law while living in a Social Compact based on equality and the recognition of unalienable rights. They had established limited governments to secure their rights. The colonists were rapidly developing the most free and just societies not only of their age, but of any time in history.

America offered its colonists a clean slate on which to write history. The First Principles were permitted to take deep root in the American wilderness. The colonies had become a great experiment in whether men could govern themselves under a free and just government, and the colonies enthusiastically responded by embracing the First Principles. Little wonder then, that when the liberties they cherished and guarded were threatened by King and Parliament, the colonies would resist English oppression and declare Independence.

Chapter 4
Revolution!

These are the times that try men's souls: The summer soldier and the sunshine patriot will, in this crisis, shrink from the service of his country; but he that stands it NOW, deserves the love and thanks of man and woman. Tyranny, like hell, is not easily conquered; yet we have this consolation with us, that the harder the conflict, the more glorious the triumph. What we obtain too cheap, we esteem too lightly: 'Tis dearness only that gives every thing its value. Heaven knows how to put a proper price upon its goods; and it would be strange indeed, if so celestial an article as FREEDOM should not be highly rated. Thomas Paine, *The Crisis, No. I* (1776).

Rebellion to tyrants is obedience to God. Benjamin Franklin (1776).

❋   Beginning with the imposition of taxes without representation, the King and Parliament oppressed the rights of colonists

❋   Following a long train of abuses, the colonists resisted British oppression and protected their liberty by declaring independence

❋   The First Principles were the motivation and philosophical framework behind American resistance to British oppression and the *Declaration of Independence*

The novel circumstances that allowed colonial autonomy and individual liberty to flourish were strongly challenged in the aftermath of the French and Indian War (1754-1763). Led by Prime Minister George Grenville, the British Empire resolved that the colonists directly pay taxes into imperial coffers to help reduce the huge debt incurred in the war – which in large part was fought to defend the colonies and expand the British Empire in North America.

When colonists resisted these taxes, on the principle that Parliament did not possess the authority to tax the colonists, Britain attacked and denigrated colonial self-rule, declared colonists subject to any act of Parliament, re-imposed internal taxes, closed colonial ports, dissolved colonial representative assemblies, reorganized colonial governments, evaded the right to a jury trial when enforcing its policies, occupied colonial towns with imperial troops quartered in colonial homes, shot colonists, and declared the colonists in a state of rebellion.

The colonists understood the Empire's oppression as a direct challenge to their Social Compact and liberties. During their struggle with the British Empire, the colonists repeatedly stressed to Parliament and King that they possessed "all the liberties, privileges, franchises, and immunities, that have at any time been held, enjoyed, and possessed, by the people of Great Britain."[98] "[F]reedom" the colonists declared "is our birth-right."[99] Great Britain disagreed. To save their liberty, the colonists invoked the final First Principle and revolted.

RESISTANCE TO ENGLISH OPPRESSION

The confrontation began in 1765 when Parliament asserted the authority to tax the colonies without their consent by passing the Stamp Act. Taxing all legal documents, newspapers, pamphlets, college degrees, almanacs, liquor licenses, playing cards, and dice, the act was enforced by admiralty courts in England without a jury. Economically, the tax was rather trivial.[100] Politically, the act struck at the heart of liberty. It trampled on the long established right of a trial by jury and violated a fundamental tenet of the Social Compact – consent as the basis of a free and just government.

After all, the very origin of Parliament had been to ensure that English subjects would not be taxed without the consent of their representatives, but not one colonist served in the House of Commons or voted for those who did. The unwritten English constitution had long recognized that only the Commons could levy taxes. The Petition of Right, approved by Parliament in 1628, for instance, recognized that "no man hereafter [shall] be compelled to make or yield any gift, loan, benevolence, tax, or such-like charge, without common consent by act of parliament." In other words, taxation required consent.

Since no colonists or colonies were represented in the Commons, the Stamp Act taxed the colonists without their consent. In response, delegates from nine colonies gathered in New York on October 7, 1765 and formed the Stamp Act Congress. The resolutions of this Congress declared that the Stamp Act violated the principle of free and just government "That it is inseparably essential to the freedom of a people, and the undoubted rights of Englishmen, that no taxes should be imposed on the people, but with their own consent, given personally, or by their representatives."[101]

Faced with vigorous American resistance, Great Britain ceased enforcing the Stamp Act. Yet the English refused to cede the principle of the matter. England would not recognize that Parliament was powerless to tax the colonists. Understanding the power of principles, after it rescinded the Stamp Act, the Parliament enacted the Declaratory Act (1766), which unequivocally asserted that Parliament had the power to tax the colonists. In fact, the Declaratory Act broadly announced that Parliament had the authority to make any law regarding the colonies. Following enunciation of this principle, Parliament would soon enact new and more onerous taxes and policies.

The British justified this assertion of authority with the contention that, unbeknownst to the colonists, Parliament in fact ruled with their consent. The colonists' interests, so went the argument, were represented in Parliament as that body represented the interests of the entire Empire – colonists and all. This doctrine of "virtual representation" was rejected by the colonists as a mere sham. John Adams explained: "we are not represented in that assembly in any sense, unless it be by a fiction of law, as insensible in theory as it would be injurious in practice, if such a taxation should be grounded at all."[102]

Yet some colonists and many English could not understand the ferocity of the colonists' opposition to the taxes. In comparison to the taxes paid by those in Great Britain proper, the colonists were still lightly taxed – the colonists appeared to be nothing more than spoiled subjects who desired the benefits of the Empire but not pay for their costs.

Americans, however, invoked the ancient governing principles of England to justify their resistance. The colonists believed that they had founded a sanctuary of freedom in the New World where the rights of Englishmen would be respected, and that even other rights, for example, religious toleration, would be secure. In fact, the First Charters of the colonies recognized that the colonists were in full possession of their English rights.[103]

John Dickinson, an early intellectual leader of the colonies' discontent, explained why American resistance to the principle of virtual representation was much more important than a few shillings. In his well read and influential pamphlets, he acknowledged that because of the minute nature of the taxes under the Stamp Act "some persons may think this act of no consequence, because the duties are so *small.*" But, he explained, such thinking was "A fatal error." He elaborated:

> This is the exact circumstance most alarming to me. For I am convinced that the authors of this law, would never have obtained an act to raise so trifling a sum . . . had they not intended by it to establish a *precedent* for future use. To console ourselves with the smallness of the duties, is to walk deliberating into the snare that is set for us. . . .
>
> We are taxed without our own consent given by ourselves or our representatives. We are therefore . . . slaves.[104]

Contrary to the beliefs of the skeptics and cynics, money was not the issue, but liberty.

Jefferson also clearly understood what was at stake. A Virginian planter and lawyer who began his political career as a member of the Virginia House of Burgesses, he explained that the colonists were fighting not for low taxes – as some revisionist historians have suggested – but for "their rights as derived from the laws of nature."[105] Jefferson, who had been unable to attend the First Continental Congress in 1774, drafted a document for the delegates to review in his absence. Later published as *A Summary View of the Rights of*

British America, this ground-breaking masterpiece not only thrust Jefferson into the limelight as a stunning new revolutionary leader, it gave an eloquent voice for much of the Revolution's ideology. *A Summary View* explained how the Stamp Act and its successors violated the fundamental tenets of just and free government:

> Can any one reason be assigned why 160,000 electors in the island of Great Britain should give law to four million in the states of America, every individual of who is equal to every individual of them in virtue, in understanding, and in bodily strength? Were this to be admitted, instead of being a free people, as we have hitherto supposed, and mean to continue, we should be suddenly found the slaves, not of one, but of 160,000 tyrants, distinguished too from all others by this singular circumstance that they are removed from the reach of fear, the only restraining motive which may hold the hand of a tyrant.

As Dickinson and Jefferson realized, recognition of Parliament's power to tax would inevitably lead to the recognition of Parliament's power to control every aspect of colonists' lives without their consent – a chilling prospect which would virtually turn the colonists into slaves. Indeed, by positing that Parliament had plenary legislative authority over the colonies, the Declaratory Act affirmed the colonists' worst fears. Washington summarized the American sentiment when he wrote that "the crisis is arrived when we must assert our rights, or submit to every imposition, that can be heaped upon us, till custom and use shall make us as tame and abject slaves, as the blacks we rule over with such arbitrary sway. . . ."[106]

Additional British actions confirmed the colonists' belief that the English government was conspiring to undermine their freedom. Other fundamental principles of free and just government were attacked. The *Magna Carta*, the founding charter of English liberty from arbitrary crown rule, had been established in England in 1215. Arising from the defeat of "Bad" King John by English barons who refused to follow the King into battle, the *Magna Carta* established that the rule of law and due process would prevail in England.

The colonists firmly believed that they too were entitled to *Magna Carta's* protections, yet they were subjected to arbitrary acts of King and Parliament that undermined the rule of law and due process. Taxes were imposed without representation, ports were unjustly closed by the *British Port Act* (as punishment for the Boston Tea Party), the people were tried by admiralty courts in England without a jury trial,[107] and colonial representative assemblies were shut down. Ignoring colonial petitions and requests for redress, Great Britain simply acted as it pleased. The rule of law appeared to have devolved into the personal desires of the King and Parliament.

Other cherished freedoms were quickly quashed. The *Petition of Right* had secured for English subjects in 1628 the writ of *habeas corpus* (which prohibited the King from imprisoning subjects without showing cause), barred the quartering of troops in private homes, and prohibited the application of martial law to citizens. Yet the King ordered troops to occupy colonial towns that were resisting England's coercive laws. Martial law had all but been declared in Boston, and on March 5, 1770 Bostonians had been gunned down by the King's troops in the Boston Massacre. British troops were also forcibly quartered in colonists' homes.

Free trade was also trampled by the British. The enforcement of the *Navigation Acts*, long a festering sore within the Empire, had become oppressive. Jefferson expressed the view that "the exercise of a free trade with all parts of the world," is "possessed by the American colonists as of natural right, and which no law of their own had taken away or abridged."[108] Colonists felt so deeply about this right of free trade that it would eventually bring the United States to a state of near war with France early in the nation's history and full-fledged war with Great Britain in the War of 1812. The British obviously held a different perspective.

Franklin aptly described the British policy in his biting and brilliant work, *Rules for Reducing a Great Empire to a Small One* (1773). In his sarcastic advice to Britain, he outlined the colonists' grievances in the guise of a suggestion of how to best drive the colonies away from England:

> [B]egin by laws to perplex their commerce with infinite regulations, impossible to be remembered and observed; ordain seizures of their property for every failure; take away the trial of such property by jury, and give it to arbitrary judges of

your own appointing . . . whose salaries and emoluments are to arise out of the duties or condemnations, whose appointments are during pleasure. Then let there be a formal declaration of both houses, that opposition to your edicts is treason, and that persons suspected of treason in the provinces may, according to some obsolete law, be seized and sent to the metropolis of the empire for trial; and pass an act, that those there charged with certain other offences shall be sent away in chains from their friends and country to be tried in the same manner for felony. Then erect a new court of Inquisition among them, accompanied by an armed force, with instructions to transport all such suspected persons; to be ruined by the expense, if they can bring over evidences to prove their innocence, or be found guilty and hanged if they cannot afford it.

Perhaps more insulting, however, was the intransigence of the British when faced with colonial petitions for redress. Franklin accurately described the English response: "the Parliament flout their claims, reject their petitions, refuse to suffer the reading of them, and treat the petitioners with the utmost contempt."[109]

Hardly a day passed without new insults to the colonists. More troops arrived from England, quartering themselves in American homes. More colonists were shipped to England to stand trial without juries. Additional arbitrary acts were issued from the crown to reduce the colonists' liberties and autonomy. Prior to this time, the English colonists had enjoyed freedom unknown in the world, and the Parliament and King appeared intent on destroying it.

Edmund Burke, who would prove to be a fierce and potent opponent of the French Revolution, agreed that the Americans' grievances to these acts were well-grounded in English law and England's actions extreme:

We have made war on our colonies, not by arms only, but by laws. . . . [E]very step we have taken in this business has been made by trampling upon some maxim of justice or some capital principle of wise government. . . . Had the principles of any of these acts been first exerted on English ground, they would probably have expired as soon as they touched it.[110]

Soon the evidence was overwhelming and the shackles too tight. In the Spring of 1774 Parliament passed what Americans quickly dubbed the *Intolerable Acts*. They closed Boston Harbor, shut down the Massachusetts Assembly, and denied the colonists the right to a jury trial by their peers. The long series of British actions, Jefferson wrote in exasperation "plainly prove a deliberate, systematical plan of reducing us to slavery."[111]

In response, the Massachusetts and Virginia legislatures called for a meeting of delegates from the various colonies to devise a strategy of resistance and reconciliation with Great Britain. Lacking only North Carolina and Georgia, the First Continental Congress convened in Philadelphia. The importance of the Congress was not lost on the colonists. *The Suffolk Resolves,* adopted by the County of Suffolk, Massachusetts on September 9, 1774 and penned by Bostonian Dr Joseph Warren, explained to the Congress the hour at hand.

Warren, a Harvard-educated physician turned fiery orator and leader, would later, on the eve of the Battle of Lexington, dispatch Paul Revere and William Dawes to warn that the British were coming. He served as the President of the Massachusetts Provincial Congress (the revolutionary government established by the colonials after the colonial legislature was dissolved by the British), and was martyred as a volunteer soldier at the Battle of Bunker Hill – after declining command of the troops following his recent commission as a major general.[112] One British commander at Bunker Hill took some solace in his death, calling Warren "the greatest incendiary in all America."[113]

The Suffolk Resolves explained that "On the fortitude, on the wisdom and on the exertions of this important day, is suspended the fate of this new world, and of unborn millions. If a boundless extent of the continent, swarming with millions, will tamely submit to live, move and have their being at the arbitrary will of a licentious minister, they basely yield to voluntary slavery, and future generations shall load their memories with incessant execrations."

The Congress took heed of Warren's admonition. On September 17, 1774, the First Continental Congress endorsed as its own *The Suffolk Resolves*. Less than a month later, October 14, 1774, the colonies promulgated the *Declaration of Resolves of the First Continental Congress*. The *Declaration of Resolves* reaffirmed that the colonists, "by the immutable laws of nature, the principles of the English constitution, and the several charters or compacts . . . are entitled to life, liberty, and property, & they have never ceded to any sovereign power whatever, a right to dispose of either without their consent." The Congress explained that "That the foundation of English liberty, and of all free government, is a right in the people to participate in their legislative council; and as the English colonists are not represented, and from their local and other circumstances, cannot properly be represented in the British parliament, they are entitled to a free and exclusive power of legislation in their several provincial legislatures. . . ." These declarations and actions served not only to remonstrate past British actions, but were an attempt to prevent further British encroachment upon colonial liberty.

The English ignored these pleas, and war tensions mounted. Indeed, King George III had long since decided "the New England governments are in state of rebellion, blows must decide whether they are to subject to this country or independent." The British troops stationed in America were growing in number, and they appeared ready to violently enforce colonial compliance with Great Britain's wishes. On March 23, 1775, Patrick Henry would elevate the crisis to the next level. A former storekeeper turned Virginian lawyer, he was credited by Thomas Jefferson with setting "the ball of the revolution" in motion. Henry would eventually become wartime Governor of Virginia and the Constitution's most impressive opponent, but at this time he was defining the cause of American independence and rallying the country to its support.

In a speech before the Virginia Convention of Delegates, Henry declared that the colonists had "done everything that could be done to avert the storm which is now coming on. We have petitioned; we have remonstrated; we have supplicated; we have prostrated ourselves before the tyrannical hands of the ministry and parliament. Our petitions have been slighted; our remonstrances produced additional violence and insult; our supplications have been disregarded; and we have been spurned, with contempt, from the foot of the throne." Henry warned that "Our chains are forged! Their clanking may be heard on the plains of Boston!" He exclaimed that the time was past for the idle chatter of peace; the country was already at war, and that war was worth the price of liberty:

> If we wish to be free – if we mean to preserve inviolate
> those inestimable privileges for which we have been so long

contending – if we mean not basely to abandon the noble struggle in which we have so long engaged . . . we must fight! . . .

It is in vain, sir, to extenuate the matter, Gentlemen may cry, Peace, peace – but there is no peace. . . . Our brethren are already in the field! Why stand we here idle? What is it that gentlemen wish? Is life so dear, or peace so sweet, as to be purchased at the price of chains and slavery? Forbid it, Almighty God! I know not what course others may take; but for me, give me liberty, or give me death!

When military confrontation erupted and then escalated at the Battles of Lexington and Concord on April 19, 1775, the Second Continental Congress found Henry right.

War for the Holy Cause of Liberty

After Lexington and Concord the leading patriots adopted Henry's declaration. Warren, for example, echoed Henry's sentiment when he wrote that "to the persecution and tyranny of [the King's] cruel ministry we will not tamely submit – appealing to Heaven for justice of our cause, we determine to die or be free."[114] A few short months later, on July 6, 1775, the Congress approved military action in defense of the rights of the colonists in its *Declaration of the Causes and Necessity of Taking Up Arms*. The Declaration, half written by John Dickinson and half by Thomas Jefferson, proclaimed that Parliament, having "attempted to effect their cruel and impolitic purpose of enslaving these colonies by violence . . . rendered it necessary for us to close with their last appeal from reason to arms." The *Declaration of the Causes and Necessity* explained that Americans were unwilling to be enslaved without a fight:

We have counted the cost of this contest, and find nothing so dreadful as voluntary slavery. – Honour, justice, and humanity, forbid us tamely to surrender that freedom which we received from our gallant ancestors, and which our innocent posterity have a right to receive from us. We cannot endure the infamy and guilt of resigning succeeding generations to that wretchedness which inevitably awaits them, if we basely entail hereditary bondage upon them. . . .

In our own native land, in defence of the freedom that is our birthright, and which we ever enjoyed till the late violation of it – for the protection of our property, acquired solely by the honest industry of our fore-fathers and ourselves, against violence actually offered, we have taken up arms.[115]

The *Declaration of the Causes and Necessity* affirmed for America what Henry had said to Virginia:

[W]e most solemnly, before God and the world, *declare*, that, exerting the utmost energy of those powers, which our beneficent Creator hath graciously bestowed upon us, the arms we have been compelled by our enemies to assume, we will, in defiance of every hazard, with unabating firmness and perseverance, employ for the preservation of our liberties; being with one mind resolved to die freemen rather than to live like slaves. . . .

A bloody year later, the colonies would be prepared to declare themselves free and independent states. By then the colonists understood well what they had only partially suspected at the beginning of their trials. They had discerned the logical extensions of the principles of freedom. They began to understand that government existed so "that every member of society may be protected and secured in the peaceable quiet possession and enjoyment of all those liberties and privileges which the Deity has bestowed upon him."[116] Moreover, on January 9, 1776, Paine's extremely powerful and influential *Common Sense* had been published, swaying general public opinion toward independence.

Thus, in May, 1776 the Town of Malden, Massachusetts could confidently "renounce with disdain our connexion with a kingdom of slaves; we bid a final adieu to Britain."[117] Within a few months all of the colonies would agree that their freedoms would only be secure if they severed all ties from the Empire, and established an independent nation upon just principles of free government. Thus, after his initial resolution was postponed from June 7, in the third session of the Second Continental Congress, on July 2, 1776 Richard Henry Lee of Virginia proposed, John Adams seconded, and Congress approved a resolution "That these United Colonies are, and, of right, ought to be Free and Independent States; that they are absolved from allegiance to the British crown, and all political connexion between them, and the state of Great Britain, is, and ought to be, totally dissolved." Adams wrote the following day that "Yesterday, the greatest Question was decided, which ever was debated in America, and a greater perhaps, never was nor will be decided among men."[118]

During the postponement of the resolution, Congress had appointed a committee of five to draft a declaration of independence: Thomas Jefferson, John Adams, Benjamin Franklin, Roger Sherman, and Robert Livingston. Jefferson, only thirty-three years old at the time, all but entirely composed a draft[119] that was revised in no minor measure by the Congress and adopted unanimously on July 4.[120] The power of the *Declaration of Independence*, perhaps the most profound political statement ever written, stems from its concise but penetrating articulation of our First Principles:

> When in the Course of human events, it becomes necessary for one people to dissolve the political bands which have connected them with another, and to assume among the Powers of the earth, the separate and equal station to which the Laws of Nature and Nature's God entitle them, a decent respect to the opinions of mankind requires that they should declare the causes which impel them to separation.

> We hold these truths to be self-evident: that all men are created equal; that they are endowed, by their Creator, with certain unalienable rights; that among these are Life, Liberty, and the pursuit of Happiness. That to secure these rights,

Governments are instituted among Men, deriving their just powers from the consent of the government, That whenever any Form of Government becomes destructive to these ends, it is the right of the people to alter or abolish it, and to institute a new Government, laying its foundation on such principles, and organizing its powers in such form, as to them shall seem most likely to effect their Safety and Happiness. Prudence, indeed, will dictate that Governments long established should not be changed for light and transient causes; and accordingly all experience hath shown, that mankind are more disposed to suffer, while evils are sufferable, than to right themselves by abolishing the forms to which they are accustomed. But when a long train of abuses and usurpations, pursuing invariably the same Object evinces a design to reduce them under absolute Despotism, it is their right, it is their duty, to throw off such Government, and to provide new Guards for their future security. Such has been the patient sufferance of these Colonies; and such is now the necessity which constrains them to alter their former Systems of Government. The history of the present King of Great Britain is a history of repeated injuries and usurpations, all having in direct object the establishment of an absolute Tyranny over these States. . . .

Jefferson later explained that the object of the *Declaration of Independence* was "Not to find our new principles, or new arguments," but rather it was "to be an expression of the American mind, and to give to that expression the proper one and spirit called for by the occasion."[121]

Patrick Henry's exclamation that America rebelled for "the holy cause of liberty" – against the freest nation in Europe – was confirmed by the *Declaration of Independence*.[122] More startling, however, is the realization that prior to America, no government in human history had been established for the purpose of protecting liberty.

America rejected the governmental shackles of the past. The Founders recognized that when their liberties had been trampled and their freedom threatened by the British Empire, that they could rightly call upon the final

First Principle – the right of rebellion. The tyrannical establishment of order was rebuked, and a new government was established to secure the unalienable rights of individuals. Jefferson aptly described the situation as one in which "asserting the rights of human nature was the clarion call of the American republic."[123] Paine frankly described the paradox to the British: "We fight not to enslave, but to set a country free, and to make room upon the earth for honest men to live in. In such a cause we are sure we are right; and we leave to you the despairing reflection of being the tool of a miserable tyrant."[124]

John Adams summarized the American experience: "What do we mean by the Revolution? The war? That was no part of the Revolution; it was only an effect and consequence of it. The Revolution was in the minds of the people, and this was effected, from 1760 to 1775, in the course of fifteen years before a drop of blood was shed at Lexington."[125] No wonder the British band played "The World Turned Upside Down" when Cornwallis surrendered at Yorktown.

Chapter 5
The Crisis

The American war is over; but this is far from being the case with the American revolution. On the contrary, nothing but the first act of the great drama is closed. It remains yet to establish and perfect our new forms of government, and to prepare the principles, morals, and manners of our citizens for these forms of government after they are established and brought to perfection. Benjamin Rush, *The Defects of the Confederation* (Philadelphia, Pennsylvania: 1787).

❋   After America won independence, the states adopted constitutions embodying the First Principles

❋   Congress was too weak to be effective in foreign policy, to prevent civil disorder, or to regulate economic activity

❋   Running amok, several states violated the unalienable rights of individuals

❋   A crisis existed regarding whether Americans would preserve a just and free society or would lapse into oppressive regimes

---

Following the Revolution, America faced the growing pains of a new nation forged on revolutionary principles. Understanding this era following the *Declaration of Independence* and prior to the adoption of the Constitution is critical to comprehending the constitutional structure under which we live. At first, the states embraced independence by establishing new state constitutions that embodied many features of a free and just society. After the Revolutionary War, however, many of these same state governments infringed upon the rights they were intended to protect. Moreover, the national government was so feeble that it could neither stop the states' abuses nor fulfill its basic responsibilities. These circumstances set the stage for the Second American Revolution – the adoption of the Constitution.

THE NEW STATE CONSTITUTIONS

With the Revolution came an explosion of political and societal reform. The *Declaration of Independence* nearly propelled the states into the original state of nature. No longer bound to King or Parliament, the thirteen states were presented with a unique opportunity to restructure their governments. "Our Revolution," Thomas Jefferson observed, "presented us an album on which we were free to write what we pleased."[126] States immediately began to create new constitutional systems, resulting in the first modern governments defined and established by written constitutions.

These constitutions embodied fundamental alterations to the structure of the state government as well as the constitutionalization of protections of liberty. The states established governments on republican principles. Legislatures and governors were elected by and accountable to free men. Nobility and royal privilege were abolished. Written bills of rights protecting individual rights were essential parts of the governing documents.

Moreover, many of the state charters recognized the First Principles. Constitutions expressly recognized the unalienable nature of certain rights, the equality of men, and the origin of just government through the Social Compact. For example, the Virginia Constitution of 1776, drafted by George Mason and adopted just prior to the *Declaration of Independence*, provided:

> That all men are by nature equally free and independent, and have certain inherent rights, of which, when they enter into a state of society, they cannot, by any compact, deprive or divest their posterity; namely, the enjoyment of life and

liberty, with the means of acquiring and possessing property, and pursing and obtaining happiness and safety.[127]

Other states drafted and ratified very similar constitutional provisions.[128]

The states clearly embraced Locke's understanding of individual rights. Not unlike the *Declaration of Independence*, the state constitutions consistently referred to the "inherent and inalienable," "natural," and "natural, inherent, and unalienable," and "natural, essential, and unalienable,"[129] rights which "cannot, by any compact, [be] deprive[d] or devest[ed]."[130] The New Hampshire Constitution of 1784, for instance, provided:

> When men enter into a state of society, they surrender up some of their natural rights to that society, in order to insure the protection of others; and, without such equivalent the surrender is void. Among the natural rights, some are in their very nature unalienable, because no equivalent can be given or received for them.[131]

In short, the new state constitutions stared down the specter of Hobbes, and enacted in their fundamental laws the First Principles for which they had declared independence.

STATES AMOK

Even while the states were taking their initial steps toward protecting individual liberties, their policies and governing structures just as often undermined their achievements. While ostensibly protecting many individual rights, the structures of many state governments were fundamentally flawed. Prior to the Revolution, the colonial governors were royal officials who often abused their power to further unjust British policy. Inherently distrustful of Kings and governors, the newly-freed states vested legislatures – assumed to be the strong guardians of the people – with the great bulk of power. Governors consequently became figureheads or nonexistent. Pennsylvania, for instance, replaced the Governor with a twelve-person Executive Council.

Many states mandated that governors be elected by the legislature for short terms, thereby subjecting the governors to the whims and mercies of the legislatures.

Similarly, the judicial branch was weak and largely undefined. Thus, state legislatures exercised not only legislative power, but often exercised or dominated executive and judicial powers. Some states even adopted single-chambered (unicameral) legislatures, leaving all power in the hands of a few assemblymen who often acted quickly upon passion rather than cautiously upon reason. Critics also charged that the state legislatures were composed of less than able politicians who were often beholden to the more unsavory elements of society.

Not only did the states vest nearly unchecked power in their respective legislatures, many appeared incapable of protecting liberty and maintaining public order. Shays' Rebellion in Massachusetts sent ripples of dread throughout the states. Farmers in western Massachusetts sacked courthouses and sparked civil disorder to protest taxes they found overbearing. Although defeated by the militia, many of the leaders of the rebellion were not only pardoned but later elected to the state legislature. In fact, many of the rebels' demands were subsequently enacted into law. In response, many political leaders across the continent became disillusioned – they had not risked their lives and fortunes during the Revolution so that mobs and civil disorder would replace Parliament and King.

Moreover, state governments all but utterly ruined the financial system in America. As the result of the Revolution and the accompanying disruption of trade with Great Britain, many indebted farmers and merchants faced dire economic circumstances. In response, several state legislatures issued nearly worthless paper money and enacted debtor relief legislation that invalidated previously legitimate private contractual arrangements. Some legislatures delayed or reduced the payment of public and private debts, refused to pay their quotas of national expenses, and raised their own salaries while lowering those of other government officials. At the same time, many creditors' debts were paid with hyper-inflationary paper money. The result was economic devastation. In a later age, Justice George Sutherland of the United States Supreme Court explained the consequences of the states' actions:

Bonds of men whose ability to pay their debts was unquestionable could not be negotiated except at a discount of thirty, forty, or fifty per cent. Real property could be sold only at a ruinous loss. Debtors, instead of seeking to meet their obligations by painful effort, by industry and economy, began to rest their hopes entirely upon legislative interference. The impossibility of payment of public or private debts was widely asserted, and in some instances threats were made of suspending the administration of justice by violence. The circulation of depreciated currency became common. Resentment against lawyers and courts was freely manifested, and in many instances the course of the law was arrested and judges restrained from proceeding in the execution of their duty by popular and tumultuous assemblies.[132]

Most Americans strongly believed in the unalienable right to property and to pursue happiness without undue government interference. Indeed, Madison observed that the "protection of different and unequal faculties of acquiring property" was the "first object" of government.[133] Pressured by debtors, many state governments broke with this tradition and placed under siege traditional property rights. Such legislation, *The Petition from the Town of Salem* (1784) explained, was "founded not upon the principles of Justice, but upon the Right of the Sword; because no other Reason can be given why the Act . . . was passed than because the Legislature had the Power and Will to enact such a Law." Madison remarked that such laws "are contrary to the first principles of the social compact and to every principle of sound legislation."[134] The legislative bodies infringed upon the fundamental rights of the citizens they were entrusted to protect. Here, Hobbes was winning.

These and other abuses of the states strongly altered the political philosophy of Americans. Prior to the Revolution, many leaders' beliefs were rooted in the classical ideals of public virtue and republicanism. These leaders believed that the public was virtuous and that the consent of the majority legitimized government action. Combined with this understanding was the belief by many that the end of government was the public good – and that all citizens were expected to further the public good.[135] Flirting with Hobbes, the revolutionary leader Dr Benjamin Rush reflected the sentiments of many at the time of the Revolution when he stated that "Every man in a republic is public property. His time and talents – his youth – his manhood – his old age – nay more, life, all belong to his country."[136] The revolutionary leader Samuel Adams stated the proposition even more bluntly: "A Citizen owes everything to the Commonwealth."[137] Thus, even his cousin John Adams could at one time declare that "a democratical despotism is a contradiction in terms."[138]

When unfettered popular state governments violated traditional rights and created unjust laws, this zeal for republicanism soon dissipated. As the unchecked will of the majority began to trample well-established property rights, those who had trumpeted unbridled republicanism began to retrace their steps and oppose it. Concluding that the actions of the state legislatures were motivated not by virtue but greed and licentiousness, Americans began to understand that unchecked state representatives of the people were to be as much feared as unbridled Kings and Royal Governors.[139] "At the commencement of the Revolution," a journalist noted, "it was supposed that what is called the executive part of government was the only dangerous part; but we see now that quite as much mischief, if not more, and as much arbitrary conduct acted, by the legislature."[140]

John Adams had remarked as early as July 3, 1776, that "The people will have unbounded power. And the people are extremely addicted to Corruption and Venality, as well as the great. – I am not without Apprehensions from this Quarter. But I must submit all my Hopes and Fears to an overruling Providence, in which, unfashionable as the Faith may be, I firmly believe."[141] With experience, the Founders recognized that faith was not enough. The tyranny of the British was being supplanted by the tyranny of the legislatures. Americans began to understand the wisdom of the warning of Montesquieu, the great French political thinker in whom most political leaders of the American Revolution had unwavering faith:[142] "Were the executive power not to have a right of restraining the encroachments of the legislative body, the latter would become despotic; for as it might arrogate to itself what authority it pleased, it would soon destroy all the other powers."[143]

Madison brought to life Montesquieu's warning in light of the American condition: "Wherever the real power in a Government lies, there is a danger of oppression. In our Governments, the real power lies in the majority of the Community, and the invasion of rights is chiefly to be apprehended, not from acts of Government contrary to the sense of its constituents, but from acts in which the Government is the mere instrument of the major number of constituents."[144] The state legislatures, John Francis Mercer declared at the Constitutional Convention, had become the epitome of the "corruption" of liberty. Elbridge Gerry similarly stated at the Constitutional Convention that while he still believed in republicanism, "The evils we experience flow from the excess of democracy. The people do not want virtue, but are the dupes of pretended patriots." Gerry admitted to the Convention that he "had been taught by experience the danger of the leveling spirit." Edmund Randolph, an influential delegate (and subsequently disgraced Attorney General for George Washington), remarked to the Convention that they had assembled "to provide a cure for the evils which the United States labored; that in tracing these evils to their origin, every man had found it in the turbulence and follies of democracy; that some check, therefore, was to be sought against the tendency of our governments. . . ."

The states had fallen from grace. While enacting the strongest protections of liberty known to man, the critical flaws of the state constitutions permitted their governments to infringe the unalienable rights of individuals. Although the states were established to protect liberty, they were threatening to devour it.

THE ARTICLES OF CONFEDERATION

The *Declaration of Independence* birthed not only the revolutionary state constitutions, but also the first continental government uniting the newly independent states. During and immediately following the Revolution, the states were loosely united by a central government established by the Articles of Association (1774) and then the Articles of Confederation (1778). The Articles of Confederation governed the country through most of the Revolution, into peace, and until the ratification of the Constitution in 1788 by nine states.[145]

The Articles' primary purpose was to unite the colonies during the war of independence, and it just barely sufficed. With the coming of peace, the fatal flaws of the Articles came sharply into focus. Fighting the tyranny of King and Parliament, the colonies were reluctant to vest the new continental government with much power. "In the commencement of a revolution which received its birth from the usurpations of tyranny, nothing was more natural than that the public mind should be influenced by an extreme spirit of jealousy. To resist these encroachments, and to nourish this spirit, was the great object of all our public and private institutions," Alexander Hamilton explained. Yet, "The zeal for liberty became predominant and excessive."[146] In short, the Articles lacked many of the vital attributes and powers necessary for a successful national government. Establishing a one-house legislative assembly, the Articles provided for voting by states, requiring nine states to pass substantial legislation – and unanimity for any amendment to the Articles. The government, while established to protect liberty, was so weak that it was ineffective in its primary and secondary purposes.[147]

Furthermore, the very nature of the Articles undermined their ability to effectively govern the nation and direct national policy. With no national executive or judicial branch, the laws of Congress could not be executed or enforced without the complete cooperation of the states. Congress, Hamilton observed, possessed no "SANCTION to its laws" because it had "no power to exact obedience, or punish disobedience to their resolutions. . . ."[148] Jefferson explained that Congress' "power was only requisitory, and these requisitions were addressed to the several legislatures, to be by them carried into execution, without other coercion than the moral principle of duty. This allowed, in fact, a negative to every legislature, on every measure proposed by Congress; a negative so frequently exercised in practice as to benumb the action of the federal government and to render it inefficient in its general objects, and more especially in pecuniary and foreign concerns."[149]

The theory underlying the Articles was fatally flawed. Jefferson observed that "The fundamental defect of the Confederation was that Congress was not authorized to act immediately on the people, and by its own officers."[150] As the Virginian Revolutionary War leader George Mason observed at the Constitutional Convention, under the Articles, "Congress represents the States and not the people of the States; their acts operate on the States not on the individuals." Alexander Hamilton similarly observed that "The great and radical vice in the construction of the existing Confederation is the principle of LEGISLATION for STATES or GOVERNMENTS in their CORPORATE or COLLECTIVE CAPACITIES, and as contradistinguished from the INDIVIDUALS of whom they consist."[151] In other words, the Articles created a confederacy of states, not a Social Compact of the people.

Indeed, each state, possessing distinct interests with regard to the major issues of the day, commonly refused to cooperate to formulate national policy. Even when such policies were developed, they could be ignored or overridden by individual states or by a block of states. The states often either refused to act in concert or failed to enforce congressional requests or edicts. Thus, the national government was all but inoperable.

Not only did the passage and execution of national law rely solely upon state cooperation, the authority vested in Congress was wanting. The Articles, for instance, did not empower Congress to extract taxes from the states or individuals. Nor could it borrow money. Instead, Congress was forced to all but beg for operating moneys from the states. Even when the states requisitioned moneys, they often failed to meet their obligations. Nor did the Articles authorize Congress to regulate interstate commerce. The result was a series of interstate trade barriers and trade wars (usually fought with excise taxes or tariffs). The states printed their own currency and possessed their own customs services.

Foreign policy was fraught with similar tribulations. Congress could not execute treaties independently, but only with concurrence of the states. Yet, the states tended to act independently of Congress and each other. Some states passed laws violating the peace treaty with Great Britain, and possessed their own independent navies to enforce contradictory foreign relations. Although Congress could declare war, it depended upon the generosity of the states to fund and wage it. In addition, because Congress was prohibited from maintaining a standing army, it relied heavily upon the state militias for the defense of the country. In fact, Congress was powerless even in the face of domestic uprisings. Congress was incapable of aiding those states, like Massachusetts during Shays' Rebellion, that faced civil disorder.

The lack of power, however, was not the only flaw of the Articles. Power was dangerously concentrated. The Articles vested what little power it bestowed solely in Congress. No executive or judiciary could check or balance oppressive congressional action. If there was planted in the Articles a seed of tyranny, it was the failure to maintain the separation of powers.

In sum, the Articles failed. First, they did not unify the nation, but led to division and political chaos. In essence, each former colony possessed most of the attributes of national sovereignty, and Congress was at their whim. Not only were the autonomous states at times corrupt, but even when virtuous they lacked the ability to unite into one nation. Second, the Articles and the states had failed to protect liberty – the very reason for the Revolution. A crisis faced the new nation – would the country unite and forge a new government based on First Principles, or would the world's one hope for freedom collapse?

Chapter 6
The Constitution

We, the people of the United States, in order to form a more perfect union, establish justice, insure domestic tranquility, provide for the common defense, promote the general welfare, and secure the blessings of liberty to ourselves and our posterity, do ordain and establish this Constitution for the United States of America. *Preamble, United States Constitution* (1789).

❋   The purpose of the Constitution is to protect the unalienable rights of Americans

❋   The Founding Fathers embraced the First Principles of the rule of law and the Social Compact by holding conventions to draft and adopt the Constitution that recognized the sovereignty of the people, established a republic, recognized equality, and created a firm and secure government

❋   The Constitution's auxiliary precautions of the separation of powers, checks and balances, bicameralism, judicial review, and the Bill of Rights are all intended to protect freedom

❋   By creating a large republic, the Constitution protects freedom by pitting factions against each other

❋   Freedom is also protected by federalism and limiting the authority of the federal government to its enumerated powers

The crisis that enveloped the new nation after the Revolution triggered a firm response. In 1787, the Constitutional Convention was called by the Congress after a consortium of states that were dissatisfied with the Articles of Confederation set the Convention in motion.[152] In the hottest summer in memory, fifty-five state delegates gathered in Philadelphia (the delegates representing their respective states, each state with a single vote).

The Convention confronted the all but overwhelming task of establishing a new governmental framework for the fledgling nation. Before the Founding Fathers lay the unique opportunity to forge a government based on a new Social Compact. Rarely had history presented a people with the opportunity to purposefully design with great care the foundation of their governmental structure. Many in the Old World hoped and predicted that the world's only significant republic would collapse into anarchy or tyranny. Madison, therefore, did not exaggerate when he predicted that the Convention would "decide forever the fate of republican government." Alexander Hamilton elaborated on the stakes:

> It has been frequently remarked that it seems to have been reserved to the people of this country, by their conduct and example, to decide the important question, whether societies of men are really capable or not of establishing good government from reflection and choice, or whether they are forever destined to depend for their political constitutions on accident and force. If there be any truth in the remark, the crisis which we are arrived may with propriety be regarded as the era in which that decision is to be made; and a wrong decision of the part we shall act may, in this view, deserve to be considered as the general misfortune of mankind.[153]

As John Lansing, delegate from New York, observed, the Convention met that challenge on September 17, 1787 by signing a document that was "totally novel. There is no parallel to it to be found." Indeed, the Convention bequeathed upon humanity perhaps the singularly most important document in history. The Constitution revolutionized government by basing it on the First Principles. Although opposing the document, Patrick Henry aptly observed that "Here is a revolution as radical as that which separated us from Great Britain."[154]

The Constitution was an exceedingly American document. Jefferson wrote that "What is practicable must often controul what is pure theory; and the habits of the governed determine in a great degree what is practicable." Thus, he continued, "the same original principles, modified in practice according to the different habits of different nations, present governments of very different aspects. The same principles reduced to forms of practice accommodated to our habits, and put into forms accommodated to the habits of the French nation would present governments very unlike each other."[155] The Constitution, therefore, is a reflection of the American character and people – it forms a government specially crafted for America to protect the First Principles embraced by the Founding Fathers.

By embodying the First Principles in the American fashion, the Constitution included a host of ground-breaking elements for a modern national government:

* a supreme law of the land adopted by the people in a written constitution

* government of limited, enumerated powers

* federalism

* checks and balances

* separation of powers

* a bicameral Congress

* a President indirectly elected by the people

* a House of Representatives directly elected by the people

* a Senate indirectly elected by the people of each state

* frequent and set elections

* elimination of hereditary offices and nobility

* written protections of personal liberty

* provision for incorporating new territories as political equals into the Union

* elimination of religious tests to hold political office

* subordination of the military to civilian authority

* division of war powers between the executive and legislature

* appropriations bills originating only in the House, and

* a process of legalized bloodless revolution through future constitutional amendments or conventions.

The Constitution would soon be amended to add to the list the protections embodied in the Bill of Rights:

* free exercise of religion

* prohibition of the state establishment of religion

* freedoms of speech and free press

* right to assemble

* right to petition the government for redress of grievances

* right to bear arms

* prohibition of quartering of troops

* prohibition of unreasonable search and seizures

* rights to due process, trial by jury, counsel, speedy trial, grand juries, and confrontation of witnesses

* prohibitions against self-incrimination and double jeopardy

* prohibition of taking of private property by the government for any reason other than for public purposes and only upon just compensation

* prohibition of cruel and unusual punishment and excessive bail

* reservation of all rights not enumerated in the Constitution to the people or states, and

* reservation of unenumerated powers to state governments.

America's embodiment of the First Principles created an unparalleled constitutional structure – majestic and thorough, yet plain and simple. Much like a clock, the failure of one small piece can shut down the entire mechanism. Only by understanding the features and elements of the Constitution as well as how they became incorporated into the Constitution can we understand how the constitutional structure embodies our First Principles and secures our freedom.

EMBRACING THE RULE OF LAW AND THE SOCIAL COMPACT

The calling of the Convention and the subsequent ratification of the Constitution brought to life two First Principles – the rule of law and the Social Compact. By recognizing the sovereignty of the people, establishing a republic, and creating a firm and secure government, America had solidly grounded the government in those First Principles.

A Convention Called, A Constitution Ratified

Governor Samuel Huntington of Connecticut remarked at the Connecticut Ratifying Convention (1788) that "Heretofore, most governments have been formed by tyrants, and imposed on mankind by force. Never did a people, in time of peace and tranquility, meet together by their representatives, and with calm deliberation frame for themselves a system of government." The country, even while facing a grave crisis, rejected the rule of the sword and embraced the rule of law. Indeed, individual states solidified republican gains through their new constitutions and the Articles of Confederation. When those institutions proved incapable of meeting the challenges of the post-Revolutionary era, Americans turned to another republican solution – the Constitutional

Convention and subsequent ratification of the Constitution by a peaceful process.

Alexis de Tocqueville, a French social thinker whose compelling description and analysis of America in the early 1800s has won him everlasting fame, explained that the Convention itself was a revolutionary event:

> [I]t is new in the history of society, to see a great people turn a calm and scrutinizing eye upon itself, when apprised by the legislature that the wheels of its government are stopped, – to see it carefully examine the extent of the evil, and patiently wait two whole years until a remedy is discovered, to which it voluntarily submitted without its costing a tear or a drop of blood from mankind.[156]

The Convention convened on May 25, 1787. An extremely impressive and esteemed gathering of men, it included governors, generals, judges, congressmen, businessmen, financiers, plantation owners, physicians, and attorneys. Jefferson even went so far as to call them "an assembly of demi-gods." While not other worldly, the Convention certainly included an astonishing array of talent and leadership that may have never been equaled before or since.

George Washington was unanimously elected its president. Washington had been the leading personality of the revolutionary war effort. A Virginian plantation owner and large landholder, he had become a military leader during the French and Indian War, one well-known for his bravery. In one fierce engagement early in his military career, two horses had been shot from under him, yet he still led his troops when his commanding officer was slain. A towering figure, he was truly larger than life. A man of tremendous character and fortitude, through almost sheer willpower, Washington led the American Army and faltering nation through a grueling war against the mightiest empire on earth. His personal charisma and immense leadership held the rag-tag army together during the terrible times such as the Winter at Valley Forge.

"He was incapable of fear, meeting personal dangers with the calmest unconcern," Jefferson wrote. "His integrity was most pure, his justice the most inflexible I have ever known, no motives of interest or consanguinity, of friendship or hatred, being able to bias his decision. He was, indeed, in every sense of the words, a wise, a good, and a great man."[157] He developed and implemented a brilliant strategy of containing the enemy and simply persevering until his forces, combined with its French allies, could entrap the British and force surrender. Jefferson explained that "never did nature and fortune combine more perfectly to make a man great, and to place him in the same constellation with whatever worthies have merited a man an everlasting remembrance. For his was a singular destiny and merit, of leading the armies of his country successfully through an arduous war, for establishment of its independence; of conducting its councils through the birth of a government, new in its forms and principles, until it had settled down into a quiet and orderly train. . . ."[158]

Washington's invaluable presence lent the Convention tremendous legitimacy throughout the nation. Several years later, after he had announced he would be voluntarily relinquishing power by retiring after two terms as President, King George III stated that Washington was "placed in a light the most distinguished of any man living," and was "the greatest character of the age." No wonder, then, that in the wake of his death that the House of Representatives passed a resolution authored by Henry Lee that summarized America's thoughts on Washington: "to the memory of the MAN, first in war, first in peace, and first in the hearts of his countrymen."

Benjamin Franklin's presence also afforded the Convention the utmost of confidence and esteem. Fellow delegate William Pierce of Georgia reflected that Franklin was "the greatest phylosopher of the present age . . . the very heavens obey him, and the Clouds yield up their lightning to be imprisoned by his rod." The eighty-one-year-old diplomat and "The American Socrates" could barely hear, but the elder statesmen's participation gave the Convention's work great credibility to the general public.

The Convention was graced with other great figures. John Dickinson, one of the early intellectual leaders of resistance to British oppression, represented Delaware. Dickinson not only authored the *Letters from a Farmer in Pennsylvania* and co-authored with Jefferson the *Declaration of the Causes and Necessity of Taking Up Arms*, he attended the Stamp Act Congress, served in the First and Second Continental Congresses, and served as President of Delaware in 1781-1782 and President of Pennsylvania in 1782-1785 (he also served in each state's legislature in the 1760s and 1770s). Although he refused to sign the *Declaration of Independence*, he chaired the committee that drafted the Articles of Confederation.

Rufus King, a Massachusetts delegate, began his revolutionary career as an aide to General John Glover. He served as a member of the Massachusetts General Court prior to serving in the Continental Congress from 1784-1787. After the Convention he would serve in the New York legislature, the United States Senate, and as Minister to Great Britain twice. He would eventually run for Vice President two times (1804 and 1808) and for President in 1816.

Charles Cotesworth Pickney of South Carolina began the Revolutionary War as a captain but ended it as a brigadier general. He served in the South Carolina Assembly from 1769-1775 and 1778-1790. After the Convention he would serve not only as a Minister and Commissioner to France, but as a United States major general. He too would be nominated for Vice President (1800) and President (1804 and 1808).

Gouverneur Morris, a delegate from Pennsylvania, served in the New York Provincial Congress, New York Constitutional Convention, and New York Assembly. He also served in the Continental Congress and as Assistant Superintendent of Finance for the United States from 1781-1785. After the Convention he served as Minister to France, United States Senator, and Trustee of Columbia University.

Roger Sherman, who began his long political career as a town surveyor, selectman, town clerk, judge, and mayor, also served many years on the Connecticut Council and Continental Congress. He would die a United States Senator. Pierce observed that he was "extremely artful in accomplishing any particular object . . . ." He contributed impressively to the Constitution by proposing the "Great Compromise" – the decision to create a Senate in which each state was equally represented and a House of Representatives that was determined by population.

Edmund Randolph served as an aide to General Washington, mayor of Williamsburg, Attorney General of Virginia, member of the Continental Congress, and Governor of Virginia. While he ultimately refused to sign the Constitution, he would be the country's first Attorney General and would also serve as Secretary of State.

George Mason, another Virginia delegate who opposed ratification of the Constitution, was a Fairfax County Court Justice for nearly forty years, and served in the Virginia Constitutional Convention and Virginia Legislature.

James Wilson, a Scottish native, began his career as a Latin tutor, studied law under John Dickinson, served as a long-standing member of the Continental

Congress, and would eventually serve on the United States Supreme Court for nine years. During the Revolution, "He spoke often in Congress, and his eloquence was of the most commanding kind. . . . His mind, while he spoke, was one blaze of light. Not a word ever fell from his lips out of time, or out of place, nor could a word be taken from or added to his speeches without injuring them."[159] Widely acknowledged as perhaps the second most influential delegate at the Convention, Wilson was an exceptional political theorist and would spearhead the ratification of the Constitution in Pennsylvania.

Alexander Hamilton of New York, however, may have brought the most talented mind to the Convention. He began his military career as an artillery captain and became Washington's indispensable aide-de-camp for much of the Revolutionary War. A veteran of the Continental Congress as well as the New York legislature, he was a superb attorney who helped form much of the early nation's commercial law. Only thirty years old at the Convention, he played a small role there – but he would become a linchpin for the ratification of the Constitution in New York, serve as the first Secretary of the Treasury, and provide the blueprint for the American financial system. He would die in a duel at the hands of Aaron Burr, then Vice President and apparent traitor to the nation.

James Madison was likely the Convention's most brilliant political theorist. Considered "the best informed Man of any point in debate" by Pierce, Madison is appropriately known as the father of the Constitution for his outline for the new government. He proved as vital to the Constitution's ratification in Virginia as Hamilton was in New York. Another attorney, Madison began his political career in the midst of the Revolution as a member of the Orange County Committee of Safety in 1775 and in the Virginia Constitutional Convention of 1776. He served in the state legislature and the Continental Congress from 1780-1783 and 1786-1788. Madison's inspired *Memorial and Remonstrance Against Religious Assessments* (1785) became the philosophical basis for the First Amendment's nearly unprecedented prohibition of the establishment of religion by the federal government and securing the free exercise of religion.[160] Madison would draft the Bill of Rights, become Jefferson's Secretary of State, and succeed Jefferson as President.

Madison and Hamilton wrote the great bulk of *The Federalist Papers* (1788) (John Jay contributed about a half dozen of the nearly hundred articles). A series of newspaper articles published in New York, *The Federalist Papers* advocated the ratification of the Constitution while explaining its underlying theories. The *Federalist Papers* were vital to the passage of the Constitution in New York as well as other states. Madison stated that *"The Federalist* may be fairly enough be regarded as the most authentic exposition of the text of the Federal Constitution, as understood by the Body which prepared and the authority which accepted it."[161] The work, however, was much more than exposition about the Constitution. Jefferson reflected that *The Federalist Papers* was "the best commentary on the principles of government ever written."[162]

Notably absent from the Convention were three of America's leading minds and revolutionaries. Two future Presidents – John Adams and Jefferson – were in Europe. Adams was serving as Minister to Great Britain; Jefferson as Minister to France. Patrick Henry, the fiery orator, simply refused to serve as a member of the Virginia delegation. Their collective absence might have been expected to cripple the Convention, but its membership overcame this handicap in the grandest of ways.

Indeed, the Convention and the ratification of the Constitution were an historical watershed. This process established the bedrock foundation for the American polity – the rule of law. The federal government would be empowered and limited by the Constitution and the laws passed in accordance with the Constitution. All individuals, including the key governing decision makers – judges, congressmen, agencies, the military, and the President – would be bound to the follow the Constitution and the laws of the land; the same would hold true of all Americans. The calling of the Convention and the ratification of the Constitution was the living embodiment of the Social Compact.

The Sovereignty of the People

The understanding that the people were sovereign was inherent in the decision to call a Convention to draft the fundamental charter of the government, as well as the decision to require its ratification by the several states. As Alexis de Tocqueville astutely observed, "Whenever the political laws of the United States are to be discussed, it is with the doctrine of sovereignty of the people that we must begin."[163] The Convention and the Constitution were both based upon the principle – previously unpracticed in modern government – that the government be of, by, and for the people. Across the globe, most rulers held power through arbitrary rule. King Louis XIV of France wrote that "Kings are absolute lords, having full authority over all people, secular and ecclesiastical." While the House of Commons in England claimed that their authority arose from the people, the King and House of Lords ruled in their own right. Discarding divine rule and hereditary titles, Americans accepted the reasoning of the Commons and embraced the sovereignty of the people. Indeed, with the Revolution came the express recognition in state constitutions "That all power being originally inherent in, and consequently derived from, the people; therefore all officers of government, whether legislative or executive, are their trustees and servants, and at all times accountable to them."[164]

Despite this acceptance of the sovereignty of the people, the states – not the people – controlled national policy under the Articles of Confederation. Moreover, an "American" people was not yet in existence. Most citizens considered their state – Virginia, South Carolina, Rhode Island – as their nation. The people were the source of legitimacy and authority for the states, but not the national government. "It has not a little contributed to the infirmities of the existing federal system that it never had a ratification by the PEOPLE," reflected Hamilton.[165]

The framers of the Constitution, however, believed that "The fabric of American empire ought to rest on the solid basis of THE CONSENT OF THE PEOPLE. The streams of national power ought to flow immediately from that pure, original foundation of all legitimate authority."[166] Thus, the establishment of the new federal government required ratification by the citizens of the nation, albeit through ratifying conventions in the individual states. Mason, as described by Madison at the Convention, explained why ratification of the Constitution by the people was essential to its legitimacy:

> The [state] legislatures have no power to ratify it. They are
> the mere creatures of the state constitutions and cannot be
> greater than their creators. And he knew of no power in any
> of the constitutions – he knew there was no power in some
> of them – that could be competent to this object. Whither,
> then, must we resort? To the people, with whom all power
> remains that has not been given up in the constitutions de-

rived from them. It was of great moment, he observed, that this doctrine should be cherished as the basis of free government.

The brilliant Patrick Henry understood the radical alteration the Constitution and its ratification embodied. As the Constitution's most fervent and insightful opponent, he crystallized the moment: "The question turns, Sir, on that poor little thing – the expression, *We, the people*, instead of the States of America."[167] Henry wished the question to be decided by having the people sovereign within their states, but the states to be sovereign within the Union. The Convention, on the other hand, decided the issue by making the people the sovereign of both the states and the Union. As Madison explained, while the states and federal government were "constituted with different powers and designed for different purposes. . . . The federal and State governments are in fact but different agents and trustees of the people. . . ."[168]

A Republic

Recognition of the sovereignty of the people not only determined the method of enacting the Constitution, but bore strongly upon the actual structure of the government. In one sense, the Founders had no choice – America would be a republic. While some nations had elements of a republic, at the time of the Convention, the world was dominated by decidedly unrepublican forms of government. In most nations, the people were mere subjects. Opponents of republican forms of government argued that empowering the people would bring certain ruin. Nevertheless, Americans, relishing the rights of the people, had no doubt that the government would be a republic. As had been expressed in some state constitutions, the American people recognized that "the right of the people to participate in the legislature is the best security of liberty and the foundation of all free government."[169] Indeed, as Jefferson exposited, there was nearly universally agreement that "Republicanism is the only form of government which is not eternally at open or secret war with the rights of mankind."[170] A government that did not acknowledge the power of the people to participate in the governing of the nation was inconceivable.

Thus, the Constitution provided that both houses of Congress be elected bodies. The people directly elect members of the House of Representatives, while state legislatures (originally) elected members of the Senate. Modeled after the Commons, the House of Representatives is the people's direct voice in government. This "popular election of one branch of the national legislature," Madison conveyed at the Constitutional Convention, was "essential to every plan of free government." The Founders believed that the most fruitful way for the citizens to participate directly in their government is through the House, with representatives chosen for short two-year terms.

Eliminating any pretense that there was a birthright to political power, the Founders rejected the hereditary model of the House of Lords. Instead, Senators were originally chosen by state legislatures. Believing that within the Senate should reside institutional memory, thoughtful deliberation, and stability, the Founders concluded that indirect election of its membership for six-year terms was the best means to meet these ends. Even under such an indirect route of election, the ultimate authority of the Senate still stemmed from the authority of the people. Hence, the Senate, in addition to the House, was considered by the Founders as a key component of republican government.

The Constitution provides that the President be elected by a majority of the electoral college. Each state has a number of electoral college votes equal to the number of its representatives in both Houses of Congress. Each state's votes are usually cast solely for the winner of the state, though each state determines the method for allocating its votes. The electoral college does not represent the majority of the voters of the nation, but rather a majority of the voters of the states as counted by the electoral college.

If no candidate receives an outright majority of electoral votes, the contest is to be decided by the House of Representatives, with each state's delegation possessing one vote. The college, therefore, has allowed for the election of Presidents who received fewer popular votes than their opponent. John Quincy Adams beat Andrew Jackson in the House after receiving fewer popular and electoral votes; more recently George W. Bush won the presidency by capturing a majority of the electoral college votes, while losing the popular vote to Al Gore. The electoral college has also elected Presidents who received less than 50% of the popular vote. Bill Clinton never received a majority vote of the people, nor did John F. Kennedy.

While the principal purposes of the electoral college were to recognize the importance of states, respect federalism, and hedge against mob rule, at the time it also had the virtue of establishing the most democratic means for choosing a national leader in the world.

The Founders also provided that members of the federal judiciary be appointed by the President upon the advice and consent of the Senate. While not directly elected by the people, the members of the judiciary are chosen by the elected President and Senate, and their authority and legitimacy are indirectly derived from the people. Moreover, as explained by Hamilton and others, the fundamental purpose of the federal judiciary is to interpret, enforce, and resolve controversies involving the Constitution and the laws passed by Congress. Hence, through judicial review, the federal judiciary has the vital role of guarding the liberty and will of the people.

The authority of all three branches of the federal government, therefore, originates from the people. Not only are the people recognized as the sovereign, the government is established on republican principles. As Mason explained at the Convention, the Constitution was not "free from imperfections and evils . . . inseparable from republican governments," but it possessed the best "form in favor of the rights of the people – in favor of human nature."

The Necessity of a Firm Government to Protect Rights: Building a Secure and United Nation

The Founders understood from the theory of the Social Compact that the survival of a republic also depended on the vigor of the government. The Social Compact must provide certain benefits to the governed in exchange for their giving up certain rights. As Gouverneur Morris stated at the Constitutional Convention, a "firm government" was essential to "protect our liberties." Perhaps the most fundamental flaw of both the Articles of Confederation and the state governments was their failure to secure the intended benefits of the Social Compact. With insufficient power, the national government had failed to protect the unalienable rights of individuals. As the Crisis that spurred the Constitutional Convention revealed, liberty was as threatened by a feeble government as by an overpowering one.

While Roger Sherman suggested at the Convention that the authority of the federal government be limited solely to foreign policy and preventing interstate conflicts, Madison countered that recent events had shown "the necessity of providing more effectually for the security of private rights, and the steady dispensation of Justice. Interferences with these were evils which had, more perhaps than anything else, produced this convention. Was it to be supposed that republican liberty could long exist under the abuses of it practiced in some of the states?" While the federal government must be limited, the drafters of the Constitution recognized that the federal government must also be sufficiently powerful within its proper realm to protect the liberties of the people.

Sherman's point about the primary duties of the federal government, however, was not ignored. Basic to the protection of individual liberty and the formation of a viable Social Compact was the creation of a unified nation that would be respected by foreign powers. After all, if the federal government were unable to protect the nation from foreign invasion or attack, the most basic rights of American citizens would be in jeopardy. Thus, the delegates began the task of nation building.

The weak and disjointed foreign policy under the Articles of Confederation brought nothing but disdain. Spain refused to recognize American rights to freely navigate the Mississippi, and the British flagrantly violated the peace treaty by their continued occupation of portions of American territories. Reflecting on this experience, Hamilton concluded at the Convention that "No government could give us tranquility and happiness at home which did not possess sufficient stability and strength to make us respectable abroad." John Jay, future diplomat and Chief Justice of the United States, wrote in the beginning of *The Federalist Papers* that the unity of the colonies was necessary to preserve peace among the states and to secure them against foreign danger. In the tradition of both Locke and Hobbes, Jay explained that "Among the many objects to which a wise and free people find it necessary to direct their attention, that of providing for their *safety* seems to be the first."[171]

Thus, the Constitution vested the federal government with the authority necessary to maintain a viable republic in a world of hostile empires. The federal government was exclusively vested with foreign policy and war powers. Similarly, it was granted the power to organize and utilize a national military to protect national interests. No longer would the foreign policy of the entire nation be subjected to the veto of a single state. The Constitution empowered America to confront hostile powers on the world stage as a unified nation.

Moreover, the Constitution granted the federal government the authority to ensure domestic tranquility. Recognizing that the peace and security of the new nation was threatened not only by foreign enemies, the drafters of the Constitution ensured that the federal government could effectively cope with domestic turmoil, uprisings, riots, and disturbances. In fact, the Preamble of the Constitution declared that the new government was formed, among other reasons, "in Order to ensure domestic tranquility," and Article 1, Section 8 granted Congress the power to call forth the militia "to execute the Laws of the Union, suppress Insurrections, and repel Invasions." The federal government, therefore, would have the authority to put down uprisings like Shays' Rebellion.

As Madison noted, the protection of liberty and unity of the Social Compact could not be secured merely by maintaining domestic tranquility and a strong national defense. Another basic attribute of a secure nation was a uniform economic system. As explored above, the post-Revolutionary Crisis ushered in a series of conflicting trade regulations and barriers between the states, resulting in economic uncertainty and chaos. The basic economic stability of individuals was collapsing under the eroding influence of inflationary paper money and internal trade wars. To unify the country, as well as to protect the financial interests and property rights of individuals, the federal government was empowered to regulate international trade, regulate interstate commerce, coin money, and hold debt. The Constitution also prohibited states from impairing the obligations of contracts, printing paper money, issuing bills of credit, and establishing internal state tariffs. The Constitution, therefore, encouraged commercial development by creating the foundation for a national market, securing public credit, creating a uniform currency, and protecting contract rights.

Madison noted in *Federalist Paper Number 10* that "the most common and durable sources of factions has been the various and unequal distribution of property. . . . The regulation of these various and interfering interests forms the principal task of modern legislation and involves the spirit of party and faction in the necessary and ordinary operations of government."[172] By vesting the federal government with the authority to regulate interstate commerce, the channels of commerce would be free from conflicting state interference and a national market regulated by a uniform federal law could exist. The Constitution unified what had been autonomous, disparate, and competing agrarian and commercial economic pockets into one market – and would eventually permit the country to become an economic giant.

The federal government, then, was empowered with the requisite powers to protect the security of its citizens while effectively uniting and governing the nation by establishing and maintaining the Social Compact.

RECOGNIZING AND SECURING UNALIENABLE RIGHTS: THE PURPOSE AND LIMIT OF THE CONSTITUTION

The *Declaration of Independence* explained that, in America, governments are instituted to protect the unalienable rights of individuals. Echoing the *Declaration of Independence*, Gouverneur Morris stated that government is "instituted for the protection of the rights of mankind," and that the Convention should secure a "plan as will be most likely to secure our liberty and happiness." George Mason similarly remarked at the Convention that the "primary object – the polar star" of the Convention was "the preservation of the rights of people." Charles Pickney joined his colleagues at the Convention when he stated that "extending to its citizens all the blessings of civil & religious liberty" is the "great end" and "object of our government. . . ." Hamilton later observed that the adoption of the Constitution was necessary to "the preservation of that [republican] species of government, to liberty, and to property."[173] Likewise, Jefferson wrote that "In truth" the establishment of a limited government to preserve liberty "is the whole object of the present controversy."[174] In short, the primary purpose of the American Constitution is to protect the unalienable rights of individuals.

By establishing a republic capable of defending the nation from foreign enemies, preserving internal peace, and securing the channels of commerce, the Founders set a foundation upon which the rights of individuals could be protected. Yet the experiences of the recent past proved to the delegates of the Constitutional Convention that a strong central government was to be feared. King and Parliament, after all, had attempted to enslave the colonists. The Founders recognized that the powerful government they created to protect liberty was itself a grave threat to liberty.

Moreover, because the government was to be a republic, the greatest threat to liberty was oppression by the majority (or, at least, the representatives of the majority). In his *First Inaugural Address* (1801), Jefferson explained the dilemma of American government when he referred to the inherent tension between republican government and the protection of unalienable rights: "All, too, will bear in mind this sacred principle, that though the will of the majority is in all cases to prevail, that will to be rightful must be reasonable; that the minority possess their equal rights, which equal law must protect, and to violate would be oppression." In other words, simply because the Constitution was guided by the polestar of liberty was no guarantee that it would protect it – the rub was in the details. "If men were angels," Madison wrote in *The Federalist Papers*, "no government would be necessary. If angels were to govern men, neither external nor internal controls on government would be necessary." Yet, the angels remain in heaven and imperfect men must govern themselves. Madison brilliantly summarized the crux of the issue: "the great difficulty lies in this: you must first enable the government to control the governed; and in the next place oblige it to control itself."[175]

Fearful that the federal government they established to protect their rights could be their greatest enemy, the Founders crafted a constitutional structure designed to allow majority rule while protecting the unalienable rights of individuals. The Constitution embodied the First Principle that the very purpose of the government is to secure rights; and that a legitimate government's authority must be limited to those powers necessary to protect such rights.

Auxiliary Precautions

While describing the crux of the difficulties of maintaining a free and just government in a republic, Madison wrote that "A dependence on the people is, no doubt, the primary control on the government; but experience has taught mankind the necessity of auxiliary precautions."[176] Madison, as the primary draftsman of the Constitution, masterfully provided for such auxiliary precautions.

The Separation of Powers

One truly revolutionary and auxiliary precaution was the weaving into the constitutional fabric the principle of separation of powers. Historically, most governments had vested the legislative, executive, and judicial powers into one person: a monarch, emperor, or king. England, on the other hand, possessed a more mixed government – vesting some legislative powers in both the King and Parliament, as well as limited judicial authority in somewhat independent courts. Yet the House of Commons was often highly subordinate to the King since he could call and disband the Commons at will. The House of Lords was the court of final appeal; much of the rest of the judiciary was beholden to the King. While the Commons possessed the power of the purse, the King held vast legislative authority.

Although some claimed that the English Constitution created the perfect mix of authority, the Founding Fathers adopted Montesquieu's theory that the separation of the legislative, executive, and judicial powers into distinct branches of government was vital to freedom. Indeed, Madison called the doctrine "a first principle of free government," and wrote that "[t]he accumulation of all powers, legislative, executive, and judiciary, in the same hands, whether of one, a few, or many, and whether hereditary, self-appointed, or elective, may justly be pronounced the very definition of tyranny."[177] For, as Montesquieu explained, "When the legislative and executive powers are united in the same person, or in the same body of magistrates, there can be no liberty; because apprehensions may arise, lest the same monarch or senate should enact tyrannical laws, to execute them in a tyrannical manner."[178]

Similarly, "there is no liberty, if the judiciary power be not separated from the legislative and executive. Were it joined with the legislative, the life and liberty of the subject would be exposed to arbitrary control; for the judge would be then the legislature. Were it joined to the executive power, the judge might have with violence and oppression."[179] Hence, "the preservation of liberty," Madison concluded, requires that the three great departments of power should be separate and distinct.[180]

The Founders separated the powers of government by vesting the legislative power into Congress, the executive power into the President, and the judicial power into the Supreme Court. To ensure their separation, each branch of government is chosen from independent sources and maintains its powers independently. No member of one branch may simultaneously serve another. Each branch possesses its authority independent of the others. Unlike most modern parliamentary democracies, the President is not the leader of the majority party of the legislature or even a legislator, but is independently elected by the nation via the electoral college. Likewise, the President's cabinet members cannot be members of Congress. Other than the extreme circumstance of impeachment, the President may not be removed by the Congress – there is no vote of no confidence or other procedure to legislatively terminate his or her leadership.

Similarly, Congress may not be dissolved by the President and he is powerless to dismiss its members. In fact, the President cannot even introduce a bill into Congress – the President's legislative proposals must be introduced by representatives or senators who support them. Representatives and senators are elected independently of the President and the Supreme Court.

Other than impeachment, Congress possesses no judicial authority. Once the President's appointments are approved, the Congress has no executive authority. With perhaps the exception of the presidential pardon, the President possesses no judicial power. The members of the Supreme Court may be neither congressmen nor executive officers. Although the number of Justices is determined by the Congress, once appointed by the President and approved by the Senate, the justices and judges of the Supreme Court and the lower courts, save for impeachment, serve for life and are independent of the Congress and President. Neither the President nor the Congress can dissolve the Supreme Court or reverse its constitutional decisions; Congress is powerless even to lower the salaries of sitting federal judges.

By protecting against the aggrandizement of power in any one branch of government, the institutionalization of the separation of powers in the Constitution furthers the First Principle of protecting the unalienable rights of individuals.

Checks and Balances

Madison also recognized that to maintain the separation of powers is a "most difficult task" which must be supplemented by "some practical security for each [branch], against the invasion of the others."[181] Indeed, only by granting each branch of government defensive mechanisms against the other branches could each branch effectively carry out its duties. At the Convention, Madison explained the necessity of checks and balances between the branches of government:

> If a constitutional discrimination of the departments on paper were a sufficient security to each against encroachments of the others, all further provisions would indeed be superfluous. But experience had taught us a distrust of that security and that it is necessary to introduce such a balance of powers and interests as will guaranty the provisions on paper. Instead, therefore, of contenting ourselves with laying down the theory of the Constitution that each department ought to be separate and distinct, it was proposed to add a defensive power to each, which should maintain the theory in practice. In so doing, we did not blend the departments together. We erected effectual barriers for keeping them separate.[182]

The Founders vested each branch with sufficient power to check the others from excesses and, at the same time, to maintain its independence and integrity. This system of checks and balances takes many forms. The President, for instance, is vested with the power to prohibit legislation from becoming law by exercising a veto (or, in the rare case of "pocket veto," by not signing a bill). James Wilson explained at the Convention that, contrary to classical beliefs, a strong executive, "instead of being the foetus of monarchy, would be the best safeguard against tyranny." Gouverneur Morris agreed that "The legislature will continually seek to aggrandize and perpetuate themselves and will seize those critical moments produced by war, invasion, or convulsion for that purpose. It is necessary, then, that the executive magistrate should be the guardian of the people, even of the lower classes, against legislative tyranny. . . ." Thus, Rufus King could rely "on the vigor of the executive as a great security for the public liberties."

The Congress, however, also possesses a balance against the President – it may override a presidential veto by a vote of two-thirds of both Houses. Congress, therefore may override an arbitrary, oppressive, or unpopular President.

The Founding Fathers also crafted into the Constitution particular divisions between the branches of government regarding the most vital (and, consequently, most likely to be abused) powers. While the President is the Commander-in-Chief of the armed forces, only Congress may declare and fund war. The President is vested with the power to enter treaties, but only with the consent of the Senate. The President has the exclusive authority to appoint the Supreme Court and lower federal courts, but only with the advice and consent of the Senate. The Supreme Court may strike down either an executive or legislative action that violates the Constitution through the power of judicial review, but Congress can strip the Court of its jurisdiction over certain cases and impeach its members. Congress is solely responsible for appropriations and passing legislation, while the President must execute such laws.

In short, the checks and balances of the Constitution provide indispensable mechanisms to protect the unalienable rights of individuals by hindering the ability of one branch of government to become oppressive or dominate the government.

Bi-Cameralism

Not content with ensuring that each branch of government was hemmed in by the others, the Founders also ensured that each branch was internally constrained. This is most evident with the internal limitations of the

Congress.[183] John Adams noted that "A single assembly is liable to all the vices, follies, and frailties of an individual; subject to fits of humor, starts of passion, flights of enthusiasm, partialities, or prejudice, and consequently productive of hasty results and absurd judgments."[184] "An obvious precaution against this danger would be to divide the trust between different bodies of men who might watch and check each other," Madison reflected at the Convention. "In this way they would be governed by the same prudence which has prevailed in organizing the subordinate departments of government, where all business liable to abuses is made to pass through separate hands, the one being a check on the other."[185]

Thus, there are two chambers of Congress. The House of Representatives is elected proportionally by population (*i.e.*, each representative represents roughly the same number of residents). The number of representatives elected from each state, therefore, depends entirely on the population of each state. The entire House membership is elected every two years. Like the House of Commons, appropriation bills must originate from the House.[186] Senators, on the other hand, are now elected by the people in each state; each state has two Senators, regardless of its population. Senators serve six-year terms, with one-third of the Senate elected every two years. The Senate has the exclusive responsibility to approve the President's actions regarding treaties, judicial nominees, and cabinet appointments. The nature of the chambers inevitably attracts different candidates, politics, and, at times, majority parties.

The composition of each chamber was understood to be essential to the preservation of liberty. The House of Representatives, John Adams explained, "should be in miniature an exact portrait of the people at large. It should think, feel, reason, and act like them. That it may be the interest of this assembly to do strict justice at all times, it should be an equal representation, or, in other words, equal interests among the people should have equal interests in it."[187] Hence, the House is intended to be the most democratic of the institutions of government and is intended to combat attempts to usurp the liberties of the citizenry by the other branches. Frequent elections are necessary to ensure that the representatives constantly embody the wishes and desires of the electorate. If it struck the ire of the populace, the entire House can be swept out in one election.

Originally elected by state legislatures, the Senate was to represent the interests of the people of each state. This system was so designed, Madison observed, to ensure that "No law or resolution can now be passed without the concurrence, first, of a majority of the people, and then of a majority of the States."[188] Although the Constitution, owing to an amendment, now provides that Senators are elected directly by the people of each state, Madison's observation – while diluted – still holds a strong measure of truth.

Just as important, however, was the conceived composition of the Senate. While the House is intended to reflect the desires of the general population, the Senate is intended to be composed of the wisest political actors the nation offers. With only two Senators per state and six-year terms, the seats are highly coveted – only the most talented and deserving should be chosen. Dickinson remarked at the Convention that "the most distinguished characters" would be "more likely to be selected by the state legislatures than in any other mode." Even when the 17th Amendment (requiring Senators to be elected by the people of the states instead of the state legislatures) was ratified in 1913, the exclusive nature of the body maintains the character of that august chamber.

Once elected, the long term gives Senators the opportunity to become learned in many key issues. The staggering of elections – only one-third of the Senate is up for election every two years – ensures stability since at least two-thirds remains in office after each election. This cumulative wisdom and institutional memory adds continuity to the policies of the nation. Compared to the House, the Senate is intended to be a much more deliberative and cautious chamber. This is vital, Madison commented at the Convention, because even the people understand "that they themselves were liable to temporary error through want of information as to their true interest, and that men chosen for a short term and employed but a small proportion of that in public affairs might err from the same cause. This reflection would naturally suggest that the government be so constituted as that one of its branches might have an opportunity of acquiring a competent knowledge of the public interests."

Perhaps more important, Madison continued, the Senate might at times be the only branch of elected government capable of halting a temporarily misguided populace from ruin. Edmund Randolph more bluntly stated at the Convention that the object of the Senate "is to control the democratic branch of the national legislature. . . . A firmness and independence may be the more necessary, also, in this branch, as it ought to guard the Constitution against encroachments of the executive, who will be apt to form combinations with the demagogues of the popular branch."

While the Senate is a republican institution, it is intended to check the House when it strays from sound policy or unjustly threatens a political minority. An eminent constitutional scholar has explained that "There is a tradition that Thomas Jefferson . . . upon his return to France, was protesting to Washington about the establishment of two houses in the legislature. The incident occurred at the breakfast-table, and Washington asked: 'Why did you pour that coffee into your saucer?' 'To cool it,' replied Jefferson. 'Even so,' said Washington, 'we pour legislation into the senatorial saucer to cool it.'"[189] The ingenious mix of Congress created by bi-cameralism established yet another safeguard of liberty in the Constitution.

Judicial Review

Another key auxiliary precaution of the Constitution is the power of judicial review. The essence of the rule of law is that the government must act within the law and the contours of the Constitution; and action in violation of the law or the Constitution is illegal and nugatory. Hamilton elaborated at the Convention:

> There is no position which depends on clearer principles than that every act of a delegated authority, contrary to the tenor of the commission under which it is exercised, is void. No legislative act, therefore, contrary to the Constitution, can be valid. To deny this would be to affirm that the deputy is greater than his principal; that the servant is above his master; that the representatives of the people are superior to the people themselves; that men acting by virtue of powers may do not only what their powers do not authorize, but what they forbid.[190]

A critical issue facing the Founders was how to address unconstitutional laws or illegal governmental action. This issue was resolved by establishing judicial review as a fundamental precept of the American constitutional order. Federal courts possess the authority to invalidate or strike down laws or actions of the Congress or President that violate the Constitution or the law. Although Hamilton predicted that "the judiciary, from the nature of its functions, will always be the least dangerous to the political rights of the Constitution," he also understood that judicial review was an indispensable power necessary to maintain the integrity of the Constitution.[191]

Another American novelty, Hamilton explained in *Federalist Paper Number 78* that the constitutional limitations of congressional or presidential authority "can be preserved in practice no other way than through the medium of courts of justice, whose duty it must be to declare all acts contrary to the manifest tenor of the Constitution void. Without this, all the reservations of particular rights or privileges would amount to nothing."[192] Indeed, he continued, the very purpose of the judiciary was to be "an intermediate body between the people and the legislature in order, among other things, to keep the latter within the limits assigned to their authority."[193] Thus, when the Congress or the Presidency acts beyond its authority, the courts have the duty to strike down such action and maintain the fundamental law of the nation.

To ensure that the judiciary did not unjustly aggrandize power, however, Hamilton cautioned that "The courts must declare the sense of the law; and if they should be disposed to exercise WILL instead of JUDGMENT, the consequence would equally be the substitution of their pleasure for that of the legislative body."[194]

Perceiving little danger that the courts would substitute their political desires for the clear dictates of the Constitution or legislation, the Founders embraced judicial review as yet another guarantor of liberty woven into the Constitution. Alexis de Tocqueville summarized the Founders' sentiments when he wrote that "the power vested in the American courts of justice, of pronouncing a statute to be unconstitutional, forms one of the most powerful barriers which has ever been devised against the tyranny of political assemblies."[195]

The Bill of Rights

Despite the auxiliary precautions described above, the Founders still feared that an oppressive federal government might coalesce and infringe the unalienable rights of individuals. The Founders understood that "there may be Danger of Errors on the Side of *the People*" to oppress others.[196] Despite the structural checks favoring liberty embedded in the Constitution, as with what happened with debtor relief legislation after the war, the passions of the day might sweep away the deeply-rooted rights of individuals. While fighting a crime wave, for example, Congress might override due process; or during war hysteria, the President might oppress the freedoms of speech, press, and assembly of political opponents.

The original Constitution approved at the Convention, therefore, incorporated many safeguards. For example, the unamended Constitution guaranteed the writ of *habeas corpus*, which provides prisoners the right to petition the courts to review the legality of their detention. The Constitution prohibited *ex post facto* laws, *i.e.*, criminal laws applied retroactively permitting the prosecution of acts that were legal at the time they were committed. Bills of attainder – *i.e.*, specific legislative acts finding individuals guilty of crimes – were also prohibited.[197] Other crucial liberties and freedoms, however, were not expressly protected. Religious liberty; the right to bear arms; the freedoms of press, speech, petition, and assembly; and the rights of due process were not mentioned in the Constitution drafted by the Constitutional Convention. Many Anti-Federalists – those who opposed the ratification of the Constitution – vigorously objected to its preterition of a bill of rights that expressly protected such unalienable rights. Jefferson, writing to Madison from Europe in 1787, explained that he opposed "the omission of a bill of rights providing clearly and without aid of sophisms for" the protection of several of the unalienable rights of citizens. Indeed, Jefferson articulated the sentiments of most Americans when he averred that "a bill of rights is what the people are entitled to against every government on earth, general or particular, and what no government should refuse, or rest on inference."[198]

At the Virginia Ratifying Convention, Patrick Henry, a leading Anti-Federalist, railed against the absence of a bill of rights: "The rights of conscience, trial by jury, liberty of the press, all your immunities and franchises, all pretensions of human rights and privileges, are rendered insecure, if not lost, by this change. . . . Is this same relinquishment of rights worthy of freemen?"[199] "You are not to inquire how your trade may be increased, nor how you are to become a great and powerful people," under the Constitution Henry chastised, "but how your liberties can be secured; for liberty ought to be the direct end of your Government."[200]

Many delegates to the Constitutional Convention, however, asserted that specific protection of basic rights was unnecessary because Congress possessed no power to infringe such rights.[201] In fact, when Constitutional Convention delegates Charles Pickney and Elbridge Gerry moved for a declaration that "the liberty of the press should be inviolably observed," Roger Sherman responded that the provision was unnecessary because the power of Congress did not extend to the press. Sherman's argument persuaded the Convention, and it promptly rejected the proposed amendment by a vote of seven states to four. In the midst of the ratification debate, Hamilton warned in *The Federalist Papers* against the adoption of specific protection of basic rights, cautioning that it was "not only unnecessary in the proposed Constitution but would even be danger-ous." After all, the Constitution simply did not confer the power to infringe in-dividual liberties, so "why declare that things shall not be done which there is no power to do? . . . [I]t is evident that it would furnish to men disposed to usurp, a plausible pretense for claiming that power. They might urge with a semblance of reason that the Constitution ought not be charged with the absurdity of providing against the abuse of an authority that was not given. . . ."[202]

Despite Sherman's and Hamilton's arguments, there was strong support in the country for a written and precise Bill of Rights because of the long English history of relying on such written guarantees of liberty.[203] Based on the English example, most states had already established their own such enumerations in their Revolutionary-Era constitutions. The suggestion that the newly-empow-ered federal government did not require a Bill of Rights did violence to the American psyche. Although the Constitution was ratified without the Bill of Rights, the ratifiers did so with the widespread understanding that amending the Constitution to include a Bill of Rights would be a top priority of the newly-established government.

Accordingly, during the first year that Congress met under the Constitution, James Madison, now a member of the House of Representatives from Virginia, introduced twelve Amendments to the Constitution. Ten of them were ratified by December 15, 1791 and have ever since been dubbed the Bill of Rights.[204]

As Chief Justice Earl Warren explained several generations later, "The Bill of Rights contains only 462 words and can be read in only a few moments, but from the American viewpoint it embraces the wisdom of the ages as divined from man's struggle for freedom throughout civilization."[205] The Bill of Rights expressly checks the power of the federal government by protecting the unalienable rights of individuals. The First Amendment declares that "Congress shall make no law respecting an establishment of religion, or prohibiting the free exercise thereof; or abridging the freedom of speech, or of the press; or the right of the people to peaceably assemble, and to petition the Government for a redress of grievances." The Second Amendment ensures that "the right of the people to keep and bear Arms, shall not be infringed," while the Third Amendment prohibits the quartering of troops in peacetime.

The Fourth Amendment guarantees that the "right of the people to be secure in their persons, houses, papers, and effects, against unreasonable searches and seizures, shall not be violated, and no Warrants shall issue, but upon probable cause, supported by Oath or affirmation, and particularly describing the place to be searched and the persons or things to be seized." The Fifth Amendment bars a federal prosecution without "a presentment or indictment of a Grand Jury," and prohibits placing a criminal defendant in double jeopardy, self-incrimination, and the deprivation of "life, liberty, or property, without due process of law." The same amendment requires that any taking of private property by the government be only for "public use" and with "just compensation."

The Sixth Amendment guarantees "a speedy and public trial, by an impartial jury of the state and district wherein the crime shall have been committed," the right to confront witnesses, and the right to counsel. The Seventh Amendment guarantees a jury trial as existed at common law, while the Eighth prohibits excessive bail or fines as well as "cruel and unusual punishments." The Ninth Amendment guarantees those rights not otherwise particularly protected in the first eight amendments, while the Tenth reserves all "powers not delegated to the United States by the Constitution, nor prohibited by it by the States . . . to the States respectively, or to the People."

The Constitution, therefore, expressly protects the unalienable rights of individuals from government oppression. These protections are integrated into the Constitution, the Supreme Court noted, because the Founders "foresaw that troublous times would arise, when rulers and people would become restive under restraint, and seek by sharp and decisive measures to accomplish ends deemed just and proper; and that principles of constitutional liberty would be in peril, unless established by irreparable law. The history of the world had taught them that what was done in the past might be attempted in the future."[206] Justice Robert H. Jackson, writing on behalf of the Supreme Court, elaborated regarding the profound effect of the Bill of Rights:

> The very purpose of a Bill of Rights was to withdraw certain subjects from the vicissitudes of political controversy, to place them beyond the reach of majorities and officials and to establish them as legal principles to be applied by the courts. One's right to life, liberty, and property, to free speech, a free press, freedom of worship and assembly, and other fundamental rights may not be submitted to vote; they depend on the outcome of no elections.[207]

Thus, the Bill of Rights is an essential part of the protections of liberty embodied in the Constitution. If the structural protections to liberty fail, the Bill of Rights still stands as a palladium for the protection of unalienable rights from oppressive federal action.

Protecting Liberty by Checking Factions

Although not specifically mentioned anywhere in its text, the very nature of the Constitution protects liberty by checking special interests. While America was destined to be a republic, many doubters argued that a democracy could not succeed in a country as heavily populated and as geographically large as America. According to classical political texts, democracy could only work in small countries like the city-states of Greece. A larger country was considered to be too diverse to be appropriately represented; and the separation between representatives and their constituents would become too great – democracy would degenerate into a corrupt aristocracy.

Yet, the Crisis after the Revolution revealed that some smaller states had become dominated by one special interest or "faction" – to the grave detriment of the larger society. In *Federalist Paper Number 10*, Madison defined a faction as "a number of citizens, whether amounting to a majority or minority of the whole, who are united and actuated by some common impulse of passion, or of interest, adverse to the rights of other citizens, or to the permanent and aggregate interests of the community." These factions – now often commonly referred to as "special interests" – often imposed laws that infringed individual liberty and created economic chaos. The negative consequences of factions were so profound that many in the Founding Generation feared that "the pestilential breath of faction may poison the fountains of justice."[208] At the time of the Convention, Madison explained, "Complaints are everywhere . . . that the public good is disregarded in the conflicts of rival parties, and that measures are too often decided, not according to the rules of justice and the rights of the minor party, but by the superior force of an interested and overbearing majority."[209]

Perhaps reluctantly, the Founders placed aside their prior faith in public virtue and began to accept the inevitability of factions. As Madison articulated at the Convention, the Founders recognized the practical reality that "All civilized societies would be divided into different sects, factions, and interests as they happened to consist of rich and poor, debtors and creditors, the landed, the manufacturing, the commercial interests, the inhabitants of this district or that district, the followers of this political leader or that political leader, the disciples of this religious sect or that religious sect." Unfortunately, Madison continued, "In all cases where a majority are united by a common interest or passion, the rights of the minority are in danger."

In *Federalist Paper Number 10*, Madison explored the possibility of controlling faction by either controlling its causes or by removing its effects. Concluding that the causes of faction were "sown in the nature of man"[210] and that the only method of suppressing factions would be to smother the freedom which gives it life, he determined that the best course would be to hedge its effects.[211] Madison, however, acknowledged that hedging such effects would be difficult because many members of the legislature would be interested parties in its enactments, and enlightened statesmen could not at all times be relied upon to chart a wise course for the nation.[212] Confronting the nation, then, was the issue of how "To secure the public good and private rights against the danger of [a faction including the majority], and at the same time to preserve the spirit and the form of popular government. . . ."

Turning classical political theory on its head, Madison concluded that individual rights could be best protected in a large republic. He noted that representatives in a larger nation will by necessity be chosen by a larger number of voters than representatives of small nations. Thus, the candidates in larger republics would be less successful in pandering to special interests, and the electorate would be "more likely to center on men who possess the most attractive merit and the most diffusive and established characters." More important, he remarked at the Convention, "in a very small state faction and oppression would prevail." This is so because small homogenous republics could be dominated by factions that were likely to unite in a common cause to oppress minorities, while the opposite was true in a large republic:

> The smaller the society, the fewer probably will the distinct parties and interests composing it; the fewer the distinct parties and interests, the more frequently will a majority be found of the same party; and the smaller the number of individuals composing a majority, and the smaller the compass within which they are placed, the more easily will they concert and execute their plans of oppression. Extend the sphere and you take in a great variety of parties and interests; you make it less probable that a majority of the whole will have a common motive to invade the rights of other citizens; or if such a common motive exists, it will be more difficult for all who feel it to discover their own strength and to act in unison with each other.

Thus, Madison wrote in *Federalist Paper Number 51*, the great diversity of America, combined with the constitutional order proposed by the Convention, would be the best security against a tyranny of faction because "the society itself will be broken into so many parts, interests, and classes of citizens, that the rights of individuals, or of the minority, will be in little danger from the interested combinations of the majority." As Gouverneur Morris reflected at the Convention: "One interest must be opposed to another interest. Vices, as they exist, must be turned against each other" to secure liberty.

By concluding that a republic could escape domination by unjust factions only in a large unified nation, Madison turned classical political theory topsy-turvy. Although not expressly written into its text, the structure of the

Constitution put Madison's theory into practice and it has become a pillar of American politics and liberty.[213]

A Government Limited to Protecting the Unalienable Rights of Individuals

The auxiliary precautions, the republican nature of the government, and the checking of factions were all significant safeguards of the Constitution intended to protect the unalienable rights of individuals. The Framers, however, were not content with simply designing a constitutional structure protective of liberty; they were also especially concerned about limiting the scope of the new government's authority.

An indispensable feature of the Constitution is the circumscribed purview of federal power. The political theory underlying the Constitution was that the jurisdiction of the federal government was limited to a few delineated powers. The unamended Constitution enacted this theory by expressly detailing the limited powers of the federal government, and the Tenth Amendment explicitly reiterated this structure by reserving to the states or the people all powers not specifically delegated to the federal government. Indeed, the Founders limited the authority of the federal government to those necessary and proper to establish a government of First Principles and to secure the unalienable rights of individuals.

Enumerated Powers

Fearing that the federal government could become all powerful, the Founders drafted a Constitution that expressly limits federal power to only a few selected areas that are specifically enumerated (*i.e.*, listed) in the Constitution. Referring to the unamended Constitution, Hamilton wrote in *The Federalist Papers* that the doctrine of enumerated powers "is clearly admitted by the whole tenor of the instrument which contains the articles of the proposed Constitution."[214] Madison explained the doctrine in *Federalist Paper Number 14:*

[T]he general government is not to be charged with the whole power of making and administering laws. Its jurisdiction is limited to certain enumerated objects, which concern all the members of the republic, but which are not to be attained by the separate provisions of any. The subordinate governments [the states], which can extend their care to all those other objects which can be separately provided for, will retain their due authority and activity.

In fact, Madison refused to refer to the federal government as a "national" one because a "national" government would have possessed an "indefinite supremacy over all persons and things, so far as they are objects of lawful government. [And] all local authorities are subordinate to the supreme; and may be controlled, directed, or abolished by it at pleasure."[215] The American system does not have a national government. This is so because as Madison aptly described, the state governments are supreme within those spheres of government over which the federal government does not possess an enumerated power:

[T]he local and municipal authorities form distinct and independent portions of the supremacy, no more subject, within their respective spheres, to the general authority than the general authority is subject to them, within its own sphere. In this relation, then, the proposed government cannot be deemed a *national* one; since its jurisdiction extends to certain enumerated subjects only, and leaves the several States a residuary and inviolable sovereignty over all other objects.[216]

By prohibiting federal authority in areas other than those specifically delineated in the Constitution, the doctrine of enumerated powers is a strong intrinsic check on the federal government. Just as the separation of powers limits the power of each branch, the doctrine of enumerated powers limits the power of the federal government.

Those powers enumerated to Congress in Article I, Section 8 of the Constitution, while vital, are few:

To lay and collect taxes, duties, imposts and excises, to pay the debts and provide for the common defense and general welfare of the United States . . .

To borrow money on the credit of the United States . . .

To regulate commerce with foreign nations, and among the several states . . .

To coin money, regulate the value thereof . . .

To establish post offices and post roads . . .

To promote the progress of science and useful arts, by securing for limited times and inventors the exclusive right to the respective writings and discoveries . . .

To define and punish piracies and felonies committed on the high seas, and offenses against the law of nations . . .

To declare war, grant letters of marque and reprisal, and make rules concerning captures on land and water . . .

To raise and support armies . . .

To provide and maintain a navy . . .

To make all laws which shall be necessary and proper for carrying into execution the foregoing powers. . . .

As this enumeration reveals, most of the powers granted to the federal government pertain to those issues that motivated the scrapping of the Articles of Confederation. The federal government was granted strong authority over foreign affairs, national security, interstate commerce, and finance. The enumeration also provided authority to enact laws "necessary and proper" for executing such powers. This very precise enumeration of powers repudiated the suggestion that the federal government was one of general authority.

Hamilton, who would eventually change his mind somewhat on the subject, explained while advocating for the ratification of the Constitution in *The Federalist Papers* that "The plan of the convention declares that the power of Congress . . . shall extend to certain enumerated cases. This specification of particulars evidently excludes all pretension to a general legislative authority, because an affirmative grant of special powers would be absurd as well as useless if a general authority was intended."[217] In short, "The powers delegated by the proposed Constitution to the federal government are few and defined. . . . [And] will be exercised principally on external objects, as war, peace, negotiation, and foreign commerce; with which last the power of taxation will, for the most part, be connected."[218]

Critical to preserving the doctrine of enumerated powers is the understanding that the enumerated powers could not serve as a subterfuge to expand federal authority. Thus, the power to tax or to spend money cannot be used to extend federal authority into unenumerated spheres of authority. Anti-Federalists opposed the ratification of the Constitution because they perceived in the ancillary powers of taxation, spending, and necessary and proper laws the seeds of a centralized government that would run roughshod over the limits of enumerated powers. A leading Anti-Federalist, "Brutus" – most likely Robert Yates, a New York judge and delegate to the Constitutional Convention – feared that the "necessary and proper clause" could be used to "annihilate all the state governments, and reduce this country to one single government."[219] Madison sharply rebuked such concerns as unjustified scare tactics:

> It has been urged and echoed that the power "to lay and collect taxes, duties, imposts, and excises, to pay the debts, and provide for the common defense and general welfare of the United States," amounts to an unlimited commission to exercise every power which may be alleged to be necessary for the common defense or general welfare. No stronger proof could be given of the distress under which these writers labor for objections, than their stooping to such a misconstruction. . . .

> But what color can the objection have, when a specification of the objects alluded to by these general terms immediately follows and is not even separated by a longer pause than a semicolon? . . . For what purpose could the enumeration of particular powers be inserted, if these and all others were meant to be included in the preceding general power?[220]

Jefferson likewise considered "the foundation of the Constitution as laid on this ground – that *all powers not delegated to the United States, by the Constitution, nor prohibited by it to the states, are reserved to the states, or to the people.* . . . To take a single step beyond the boundaries thus specially drawn around the powers of Congress, is to take possession of a boundless field of power, no longer susceptible of any definition."[221]

That the Founders believed the doctrine of enumerated powers was critical to the preservation of liberty cannot be doubted. Efforts to enact even clearly beneficial laws were rejected if in violation of the doctrine. President Madison's last official act, for instance, was the veto of the Bonus Bill. This law would have set aside $1,500,000 as a permanent fund for internal improvements. Madison vetoed the measure because he concluded that it was an unconstitutional action beyond the enumerated powers of the federal government. Madison reasoned that "The legislative powers vested in Congress are specified and enumerated . . . and it does not appear that the power proposed to be exercised by the bill is among the enumerated powers, or that it falls by any just interpretation within the power to make laws necessary and proper for carrying into execution those or other powers vested by the Constitution in the Government of the United States."[222] "'The power to 'regulate commerce among the several States,'" he explained, "can not include a power to construct roads and canals, and to improve the navigation of water courses in order to facilitate, promote, and secure such a commerce without a latitude of construction departing from the ordinary import of the terms. . . ."[223] Again he rebuked suggestions that the Constitution granted Congress general legislative power:

> To refer to the power in question to the clause "to provide for the common defense and general welfare" would be contrary to the established and consistent rules of interpretation, as rendering the special and careful enumeration of powers which follow the clause nugatory and improper. Such a view of the Constitution would have the effect of giving to Congress a general power of legislation instead of the defined and limited one hitherto understood to belong to them, the terms "common defense and general welfare" embracing every object and act within the purview of a leg-

islative trust. It would have the effect of subjecting both the Constitution and the laws of the several States in all cases not specifically exempted to be superseded by laws of Congress. . . .[224]

Similarly, President Monroe vetoed the Cumberland Road Bill because he found that power to provide for internal improvements "can not be derived from" the Constitution.[225]

With a few very notable exceptions, at the birth of the republic, this understanding that the role of the federal government should remain limited to a small but crucial sphere of authority remained nearly unchallenged. While granted the powers necessary to unite and govern the nation, the role of the federal government was minute during the first generations of the new nation. Fearing an overbearing federal government, the Founders limited its enumerated powers to those necessary and proper to establishing a federal government of First Principles. By limiting the authority of the federal government to its enumerated powers, this doctrine became a keystone of American liberty.

Federalism

In one sense the mirror image of the doctrine of enumerated powers, federalism provides that the powers not exclusively vested in the federal government are reserved to the states. Madison explained in *The Federalist Papers* that "In the new government, as in the old, the general powers are limited . . . the States, in all unenumerated cases, are left in the enjoyment of their sovereign and independent jurisdiction."[226] "The federal and State governments," Madison reflected, are in fact but different agents and trustees of the people, constituted with different powers and designed for different purposes."[227]

Although in adopting the Constitution the state governments lost many powers essential to sovereign nations, they retained their authority involving local governance. In fact, as intended by the Founding Fathers, federalism leaves to the states most of the areas of government that are of daily and close concern to Americans. While the powers enumerated to the federal government were precise and few, "Those which are to remain in the State governments are numerous and indefinite. [And] will extend to all the objects which, in the ordinary course of affairs, concern the lives, liberties, and properties of the people, and the internal order, improvement, and prosperity of the State."[228] Nearly all criminal and civil law falls within the province of states. Education was exclusively a state concern for generations. Except for interstate commerce, the regulation of most economic activities was intended to remain within the province of the states. Legislation involving society, culture, morality, criminal activity, and the general welfare fell within the exclusive province of the states.

Some delegates at the Convention, such as Gouverneur Morris, however, referred to "State attachments and state importance" as the "bane of this country," and argued that the authority of the states be extremely limited. Charles Pickney, for example, moved that "the national legislature should have authority to negative all laws which they should judge to be improper" because "such a universality of the power was indispensably necessary to render it effectual." Madison even seconded the motion.

Such efforts, however, were quickly rebuffed by advocates of a limited central government. Federalism, the Convention determined, is as essential to preserving liberty as is the separation of powers, checks and balances, and bi-cameralism. Madison, rejecting his earlier instinct to weaken the state governments, explained that dividing authority between the states and federal government is vital to securing freedom:

> In the compound republic of America, the power surrendered by the people is first divided between two distinct governments, and then the portion allotted to each subdivided among distinct and separate departments. Hence a double security arises to the rights of the people. The different governments will control each other, at the same time that each will be controlled by itself.[229]

Jefferson even went so far as to write that federalism is the best guarantor of liberty:

> But the true barriers of our liberty in this country are our State governments; and the wisest conservative power ever

contrived by man, is that of which our Revolution and present government found us possessed. Seventeen distinct States, amalgamated into one as to their foreign concerns, but single and independent as to their internal administration, regularly organized with legislature and governor resting on the choice of the people, and enlightened by a free press, can never be so fascinated by the arts of one man, as to submit voluntarily to his usurpation.[230]

Those who think otherwise, Hamilton commented, "ought to at least prove to us that it is easier to subvert the liberties of . . . millions of people, with the advantage of local governments to head their opposition, than of . . . people who are destitute of that advantage."[231]

The Founders constructed an appropriate and necessary balance of power between the state and federal powers. They, in fact, were so confident of this balance, that they repeatedly dismissed suggestions that the federal government would become dominant. Hamilton wrote that "It will always be far more easy for the state governments to encroach upon the national authorities than for the national government to encroach upon the State authorities,"[232] and that "It may safely be received as an axiom in our political system that the State governments will, in all possible contingencies, afford complete security against invasions of the public liberty by the national authority."[233]

In short, liberty was to be secured by the division of authority among the states and the federal government. Concentrating all authority in a national government would have allowed a pernicious President and Congress to oppress the entire nation in every aspect of government. By dividing governmental authority among the several states and the federal government, federal tyranny can be combated by the states.

Even if it arose, federal oppression would be limited to the scope of its authority. To dominate all aspects of government, an oppressor must capture all three branches of the federal government as well as all the three branches of each state government – a very difficult proposition. If tyranny springs from the state capital, one can look to the federal government for succor. If tyranny springs from the federal government, one can defend freedom with the aid of the state government. If both become tyrannical, one can flee to another state. As the mirror image of the doctrine of enumerated powers, federalism not only limits the authority of the federal government to the protection of unalienable rights, it also protects such rights by dividing the authority of government among the federal and state governments.

Federalism is also essential to the First Principle of the Social Compact. The essence of a republic is the ability of the governed to choose their representatives and hold them directly accountable for the decisions they make. If self-government is to have substantive and practical meaning, citizens must have a strong and direct influence on those vested with the authority to address issues. Thus, holding decision makers who affect local issues directly accountable to local voters is essential to the Social Compact. Moreover, only by participating in and influencing local decisions can citizens fulfill the promise of republican government and self-rule. By empowering local officials to address local problems, federalism maintains the Social Compact.

The Social Compact is compromised, on the other hand, when any local problem is addressed by a distant, nearly unaccountable government. As one Anti-Federalist explained, "in a republic of the extent of this continent, the people in general would be acquainted with very few of their rulers: the people at large would know little of their proceedings, and it would be extremely difficult to change them."[234] Under such circumstances, national decision making regarding local issues all but renders moot the Social Compact. For example, if Congress were to legislate regarding a problem facing only Michigan, the Michigan voters would be denied their right to fully participate in that decision. After all, their Congressmen and two Senators would be pitted against the entire nation. Michigan voters have no formal influence over Congressmen and Senators from Illinois, California, Texas, South Carolina, or Iowa. Thus, self-government is effectively destroyed when state problems are solved by central governments.

If governmental authority is diagrammed as a pyramid, municipal governments form a wide base, counties form the next (and narrower) level, states the next (and even narrower) level, and the federal government the capstone. When problems originating at the lower levels of the pyramid are addressed by the top, the authority of the voters on the lower levels (and the accountability of the decision makers) is diluted and the Social Compact is compromised. Federalism, by requiring state issues to be resolved by the states, maintains the Social Compact.

Moreover, federalism is simply good governance. Elbridge Gerry remarked at the Convention that "The states . . . have different interests and are ignorant of each other's interests." Oliver Ellsworth similarly commented at the Convention that "The states are the best judges of the circumstances and temper of their own people." In other words, local officials are more knowledgeable of the issues they face and more capable of resolving such issues than are politicians elected across the nation. New Yorkers simply have a better grasp of the issues facing New York than a Congress made up of representatives and senators from Tennessee, Maine, North Dakota, Rhode Island, Virginia, Wyoming, Nevada, Georgia, Oregon, and every other state. Because the interests, customs, and problems of the people of each state are unique, uniform laws regulating the people of New Hampshire, Pennsylvania, Mississippi, Wisconsin, Kansas, Hawaii, Colorado, Florida, Montana, Ohio, and Alaska either prove incompetent or onerous. Thus, good governance requires local solutions to local problems. The problems facing fishermen in Massachusetts, bankers in Chicago, manufacturers in Detroit, scientists in North Carolina, farmers in Idaho, and cattlemen in Oklahoma are different and, therefore, presumably require different legislative approaches.

Only pressing national issues like defense and interstate commerce, the Founders determined, can be competently resolved by federal legislation. Jefferson wrote that "Were not this great country already divided into states, that division must be made, that each might do for itself what concerns itself directly, and what it can so much better do than a distant authority. . . . *Were we directed from Washington when to sow & when to reap, we should soon want bread.* It is this partition of cares, descending in gradation from general to particular, that the mass of human affairs may be best managed for the good and prosperity of all."[235]

Moreover, because each state possesses the authority to legislate in its domain, each serves as a laboratory for approaches to addressing different issues. The same issue can be addressed differently by each of the several states. For example, states can take a variety approaches to education. One might choose to toughen testing standards or loosen them, implement schools of choice or busing, encourage charter schools, or award vouchers. Some reforms might work well, while others might not work at all; others might work only in rural (or more urban) states. In any event, the citizens of each state would be free to determine the best solution for them. Not only can local issues be resolved more effectively by the state legislators, but some states might find solutions that are more effective across the nation. By permitting each state to experiment with different approaches to the same problem, better solutions applicable (and adaptable) to other states could be developed. Federal legislation, on the other hand, imposes a uniform, inflexible standard solution throughout the entire nation, thereby stifling innovation and reform.

Federalism also furthers freedom by allowing families to seek the community best suited to their particular needs. Internal migration is a hallmark of American society. New York City, Los Angeles, Chicago, Detroit, Houston, Seattle, and many other communities have at one time or another attracted tens of thousands of Americans away from their home states. Different state policies attract different types of individuals and families. Oppressive or stagnant state policies or conditions result in population shifts to the more dynamic or proactive states. In fact, some former population magnets have become net emigration centers. This intra-national migration forces the states to become more accountable and, in essence, compete for population and business.

Paired with enumerated powers, federalism became a cornerstone of American liberty. Authority was not only divided between departments of the federal government, but between the states and the federal government. Hemmed in by the twin doctrines of enumerated powers and federalism, the federal government was intended to ably govern in crucial but purposefully limited areas. Enumerated powers and federalism not only limit the authority of the federal government to protecting the unalienable rights of individuals, they reinforce the Social Compact by ensuring that local issues are resolved locally. The constitutional structure allowing for the development of a free and just government based on First Principles was complete.[236]

THE POLITICAL MASTERPIECE: A RISING SUN

Benjamin Franklin remarked during the early meetings of the Convention that the delegates had been "groping, as it were, in the dark, to find political truth, and scarce able to distinguish it when presented to us." Yet Madison was able to report at the end of the Convention that when the last delegates were signing the Constitution, "Doctor Franklin looking towards the

President's chair, at the back of which a rising sun happened to be painted, observed to a few members near him, that painters had found it difficult to distinguish in their art a rising from a setting sun. 'I have,' said he, 'often and often in the course of session, and the vicissitudes of my hopes and fears as to its issue, looked at that sun behind the President without being able to tell whether it was rising or setting; but now at length I have the happiness to know that it is a rising, and not a setting, sun."

Similarly, despite his initial misgivings, in the end Jefferson could likewise confidently proclaim that "The Constitution . . . is unquestionably the wisest ever yet presented to men."[237] "We can no longer say there is nothing new under the sun," he wrote, "For this whole chapter in the history of man is new."[238] Undeniably, by embodying the First Principles of a free and just government, the Constitution illuminated the political landscape like no previous creation of man.

Chapter 7
Extending the Blessings of Liberty to All Races

What, to the American slave, is your Fourth of July? I answer: a day that reveals to him, more than all other days in the year, the gross injustice and cruelty to which he is the constant victim. To him, your celebration is a sham; your boasted liberty, an unholy license; your national greatness, swelling vanity; your sounds of rejoicing are empty and heartless; your denunciation of tyrants, brass-fronted impudence; your shouts of liberty and equality, hollow mockery; your prayers and hymns, your sermons and thanksgivings, with all your religious parade and solemnity, are, to Him, mere bombast, fraud, deception, impiety, and hypocrisy – a thin veil to cover up crimes which would disgrace a nation of savages. Frederick Douglass, *Independence Day Speech at Rochester, New York* (1852).

❋ For the Founding Fathers, equality, the Social Compact, and the recognition and protection of unalienable rights had been mostly limited to whites. However, animated by the First Principles of free and just government, America abolished slavery, extended the franchise to all races, provided for equal protection of the law, and enacted civil rights legislation

❋ Although the civil rights struggle is incomplete, inspired by our First Principles, the nation is dedicated to its fulfillment

---

While America had won its independence and established a free and just government for its citizens, it denied freedom and equality to many of its own residents – the slaves held in bondage. The existence of slavery was in direct violation of the First Principles of equality, the protection of unalienable rights, and the Social Compact. This clash between the principles of American government and harsh reality culminated in the Civil War and the emancipation of the slaves. Many decades would pass, however, before African Americans and other racial minorities would begin to approach authentic equality under the law. Along the way, this conflict bore some of America's brightest – and darkest – moments. Even now, America is clearly not free from its legacy of racial oppression.

The struggle for racial equality has a long and complex history to which this work is unable to do justice.[239] The purpose of this Chapter, however, is not to recount the historical figures or circumstances that liberated the slaves and have moved our society towards racial equality, but to reveal how our First Principles laid the foundation by which the struggle for equality became inevitable.

SLAVERY IN THE LAND OF THE FREE

Throughout the years leading to independence, revolutionary leaders justified their actions in stark terms of freeing themselves from impending tyranny. "*Those* who are *taxed* without their own consent expressed by themselves or their representatives," proclaimed John Dickinson, "are *slaves. We are taxed* without our consent expressed by ourselves or representatives. *We* are therefore – SLAVES."[240] John Adams, in his trademark sharp fashion, wrote that the colonists under English rule were "the most abject sort of slaves."[241]

That in the midst of these freedom fighters were slaveholders, of course, was rank hypocrisy. Jefferson admitted that "The whole commerce between master and slave is a perpetual exercise of the most boisterous passions, the most unremitting despotism on the one part, and degrading submission on the other."[242] Moreover, the slavery perpetrated by the colonists was more dreadful than anything imaginable under British rule. Mostly plantation workers, slaves were whipped, beaten, chained, and murdered. Slavery tore families asunder and trampled human dignity. The slaves could be rightly described by David Walker as "the most degraded, wretched, and abject set of beings that ever lived since the world began."[243]

Walker, an abolitionist son of a slave father and free mother, exposed the obvious in 1829: "our miseries and wretchedness [occur] in this *Republican Land of Liberty!!!!!*"[244] In fact, the Constitution – the document secured to protect the liberty of Americans – explicitly recognized the existence, if not the propriety, of slavery. As a matter of political necessity – actually political survival – the newly-born republic would not be free for all of its inhabitants until after the Civil War. Frederick Douglass, an escaped slave who became one of the most influential abolitionists through his newspaper and autobiography, would follow Walker's example by attacking the "peculiar institution." Douglass – who eventually bought his freedom with the proceeds of anti-slavery lectures he presented in Great Britain and Ireland – would in due time recruit African American regiments during the Civil War, serve as U.S. Marshal for the District of Columbia, and share counsel with Lincoln during the Civil War. He could rightfully ask at a Fourth of July address held over fifty years after the *Declaration of Independence*: "What have I, or those I represent, to do with your national independence? Are the great principles of political freedom and of natural justice, embodied in the *Declaration of Independence*, extended to us?"[245]

Slaves were simply not the beneficiaries of the First Principles. The unalienable rights of slaves were denied, while the rights of their masters to keep them in bondage were defended. The foundation of slavery was inequality, and slaves were excluded from the Social Compact. The end of government was not to protect the rights of slaves, but to protect the right of others to rule over them. America claimed to be founded on the First Principles of a free and just government, yet slavery made a mockery of such principles.

THE MOVEMENT TO ABOLISH SLAVERY

Although the original Constitution did not emancipate the slaves, the government it created and the ideological foundation on which it was based inevitably forced slavery's abolition. The incongruity of slavery in a free land established on the First Principles of a free and just government was simply too stark to continue perpetually. In fact, even before the *Declaration of Independence*, patriots recognized that those agitating for liberty from England were oppressors at home. "Blush ye pretended votaries for freedom!" chastised the Baptist minister and pamphleteer John Allen at the beginning of America's confrontation with Britain:

> ye trifling patriots! who are making a vain parade of being advocates for the liberties of mankind, who are thus making a mockery of your profession by trampling on the sacred natural rights and privileges of Africans; for while you are fasting, praying, nonimporting, nonexporting, remonstrating, resolving, and pleading for a restoration of your charter rights, you at the same time are continuing this lawless, cruel, inhuman, and abominable practice of enslaving your fellow creatures. . . .[246]

Benjamin Rush, the Philadelphia physician who helped spur the Revolution in that city, warned "Ye advocates for American liberty. . . . The plant of liberty is of so tender a nature that it cannot thrive long in the neighborhood of slavery."[247]

Jefferson, a slave owner, clearly recognized the hypocrisy of America's situation, and his original draft of the *Declaration of Independence* included a scathing attack upon slavery and the slave trade:

> [The King] has waged cruel war against human nature itself, violating its most sacred rights of life and liberty in the persons of a distant people who never offended him, captivating and carrying them into slavery in another hemisphere. . . . This piratical warfare, the opprobrium of infidel powers, is the warfare of the CHRISTIAN king of Great Britain.[248]

Two southern states, however, required the elimination of the passage from the *Declaration of Independence*. While Jefferson's condemnation was deleted, the grand contradiction in American life remained.

Although Jefferson lost the battle over this favored passage, he in essence won the war by including in the *Declaration of Independence* the proclamation that "all men are created equal." With the *Declaration of Independence's* acknowledgment of the equality of all men, slavery came under accelerated and fierce attack in the new republic. The idea of equality let loose by the Revolution tore down historic social hierarchies, including the landed gentry and their networks of patronage, and replaced them with liberty, equality, and republicanism. Prior to the Revolution, the King and nobility ruled – everyone else was simply a subject. The revolutionary ideal of equality, however, broke down such presuppositions and permitted men to advance with regard to their merit, not the social status into which they had been born.

David Ramsay, a contemporary historian of the American Revolution and two-time delegate to the Continental Congress, observed as early as 1778 that "Equality, the life and soul of commonwealths, cuts off all pretensions to preferment, but those which arise from extraordinary merit. . . ." Thus, Ramsay could continue, "It is the happiness of our present constitution, that all offices lie open to men of merit, of whatever rank or condition; and that even the reins of state may be held by the son of the poorest man, if possessed of abilities equal to the important station."[249]

While political expediency prevented the abolition of slavery prior to independence, the institution continued to be assaulted afterward. Delegates on the floor of the Constitutional Convention attacked slavery as contrary to the ideals upon which America had fought for independence. George Mason, for instance, observed that "Every master of slaves is born a petty tyrant." Madison similarly remarked that "We have seen the mere distinction of color made in the most enlightened period of time a ground of the most oppressive dominion ever exercised by man over man."

Slaves too were aware of not only their bondage, but of the hypocrisy of their masters. In fact, some slaves petitioned for their freedom based on the First Principles that drove the Revolution. Just as the colonists were throwing off the shackles of British tyranny, *The Petition of a Great Number of Blacks of this Province who by Divine Permission are held in a State of Slavery within the Bowels of a Free Christian Country* explained in 1774 that their slavery was in violation of the First Principles:

> [Y]our Petitioners apprehend we have in common with all other men a natural right to our freedoms without Being deprived of them by our fellow men as we are freeborn People

and have never forfeited this Blessing by any compact or agreement whatever. But we were unjustly dragged by the cruel hand of power from our dearest friends and some of us stolen from the bosoms of our tender Parents and from a Populous Pleasant and plentiful country and Brought hither to be made slaves for Life in a Christian land.[250]

In 1843, Henry Highland Garnet, a former slave, represented a growing and vocal abolitionist movement in his *Call to Rebellion*. The *Call* explained that "The gross inconsistency of a people holding slaves, who had themselves 'ferried o'er the wave' for freedom's sake, was too apparent to be entirely overlooked. The voice of Freedom cried, 'Emancipate your slaves.'"[251] Frederick Douglass illuminated a decade later that "To drag a man in fetters into the grand illuminated temple of liberty, and call upon him to join you in joyous anthems, were inhuman mockery and sacrilegious irony."[252] His unrelenting attacks upon slavery clearly revealed the need to address the fundamental contradiction of slavery in America:

> Would you have me argue that man is entitled to liberty? That he is the rightful owner of his own body? You have already declared it! Must I argue the wrongfulness of slavery? . . . How should I look today, in the presence of Americans, dividing and subdividing a discourse, to show that men have a natural right to freedom? . . . There is not a man beneath the canopy of heaven that does not know that slavery is wrong for him.[253]

Garnet echoed Patrick Henry: "Fellowmen! Patient suffers! behold your dearest rights crushed to the earth! See your sons murdered, and your wives, mothers and sisters doomed to prostitution. In the name of the merciful God, and by all that life is worth, let it no longer be a debatable question, whether it is better to choose *liberty* or *death*." Indeed, Garnet commanded, "You had far better all die – *die immediately*, than live slaves, and entail your wretchedness upon your posterity."[254]

While abolitionists demanded freedom, the ruling regime in the South was unrelenting in its defense of the peculiar institution. In fact, over time slavery spread into some newly-established states. The Supreme Court aided and abetted the cause of slavery in its infamous *Dred Scott* decision.[255] Disregarding generations of understanding of congressional authority over slavery, the Court found that Congress could not prohibit slave owners from bringing their slaves into the territories. Accordingly, the threat of slavery expanding beyond the South became a reality.

Driven by the First Principles, whether slavery would spread, halt, or be abolished became the dominating issue of American politics in the 1840s-1860s. America's choice was stark but simple: embrace the First Principles of free and just government or succumb to the dark principles of oppression. The conflict, held off for forty years by the Missouri Compromise of 1820 (permitting slavery's extension only into the Southern territories) came to a climax over the territories of Kansas and Nebraska. A shooting war broke out over the slavery issue in Kansas in the mid-1850s, and the nation's fracture line over slavery – between North and South – ruptured. When Abraham Lincoln won the presidency in 1860 on an anti-slavery platform without a single electoral vote from the South, the Southern states seceded. The drive to liberate the slaves pursuant to America's First Principles had broken the nation in two.

EMANCIPATION

When considering the tragedy of slavery, Jefferson wrote that "can the liberties of a nation be thought secure when we have removed their only firm basis, a conviction in the minds of the people that these liberties are a gift of God? That they are not to be violated but with his wrath? Indeed, I tremble for my country when I reflect that God is just: that his justice cannot sleep forever. . . ."[256] At the Constitutional Convention, George Mason similarly foresaw that the failure to abolish slavery would "bring the judgment of Heaven on a country. As nations cannot be rewarded or punished in the next world, they must be in this. By an inevitable chain of causes and effects. Providence punishes national sins by national calamities."

With the secession of the South, Jefferson's and Mason's warnings became prophecy. The Civil War began in 1861 and claimed the lives of over 600,000 Americans. Abraham Lincoln, "the son of the poorest man," led the nation through the national calamity. A brilliant lawyer in Illinois, he began his political career losing a race for the state legislature in 1832. He would win two years later and serve in the Illinois House from 1834-1841. While winning a seat to Congress in the House of Representatives in 1847, he lost his bid for reelection as well as two bids for the Senate in 1855 and 1858. Lincoln, however, was nothing if not persistent. This repeat loser won the presidency in 1860. With an uncanny intellect and will he became the rock upon which the Union was preserved.

With President Lincoln came an understanding and eventual institutional recognition of the equality of all men in accordance with the promise of the *Declaration of Independence* and our First Principles. Lincoln explained that the authors of the *Declaration of Independence* had "intended to include *all* men." The Founders, Lincoln stated:

> did not mean to assert the obvious untruth, that all men were then actually enjoying that equality, nor yet that they were about to confer it, immediately, upon them. In fact, they had no power to confer such a boon. They meant simply to declare the right, so that the enforcement might follow as fast as circumstances should permit. They meant to set to set up a standard maxim for free society, which should be familiar to all, and revered by all; constantly looked to, constantly labored for, and even though never perfectly attained, constantly approximated, and thereby constantly spreading and deepening its influence, and augmenting the happiness and value of life to all people of all colors everywhere.[257]

"Our republican robe," Lincoln lamented, "is soiled, and toiled in the dust. Let us repurify it. Let us turn and wash it white, in the spirit, if not the blood, of the Revolution." In 1854, Lincoln pleaded to the nation that it should "re-adopt the *Declaration of Independence*, and, with it, the practices and policy which harmonize with it. Let north and south – let all Americans – let all lovers of liberty everywhere join the great and good work. If we do this, we shall not only have saved the Union; but we shall have so saved it, as to make, and to keep it, forever worthy of the saving."[258]

Lincoln's plea was unheeded until our nation was divided and the Civil War engaged. In fact, the true turning point did not occur until Lincoln promulgated the *Emancipation Proclamation* on New Year's Day, 1863. Having struggled to find a capable leader of the Union's troops for much of the war, Lincoln only revealed his plans for emancipation after General George McClellan won a Union victory at Antietam in September of 1862. Declaring all slaves in states under the South's control to be free, the Proclamation was barely rooted in the First Principles of free and just government. Its text justified the freeing of the slaves on military grounds. In fact, by securing European support for the North, the Proclamation was as much a brilliant strategic move on the battlefield as a blow for freedom.

The higher purposes underlying the Proclamation would not find voice until eleventh months later. Lincoln's *Gettysburg Address* (1863) was a defining moment in the struggle to secure equality and liberty for all Americans. While possessing no legal authority, it is nearly as important to the American character as the *Declaration of Independence*. No other speech reveals – and helped cause – the evolution of American thought. In perhaps the most famous speech in American history, Lincoln explained that America was founded upon certain First Principles and that it must struggle to meet those principles – even at great and horrible costs – to ensure that the nation dedicated to those principles would survive:

> Four score and seven years ago, our fathers brought forth on this continent a new nation, conceived in liberty and dedicated to the proposition that all men are created equal.

> Now we are engaged in a great civil war, testing whether that nation or any nation so conceived and so dedicated, can long endure. We are met on a great battlefield of that war. We have come to dedicate a portion of that field, as a final resting place for those who here gave their lives that the nation might live. It is altogether fitting and proper that we should do this.

> But, in a larger sense, we can not dedicate – we can not consecrate – we can not hallow – this ground. The brave men,

living and dead, who struggled here, have consecrated it, far above our poor power to add or detract. The world will little note, nor long remember what we say here, but it can never forget what they did here. It is for us the living, rather, to be dedicated here to the unfinished work which they who fought here have thus so far nobly advanced. It is rather for us to be here dedicated to the great task remaining before us – that from those honored dead we take increased devotion to that cause for which they gave the last full measure of devotion – that we here highly resolve that these dead shall not have died in vain – that this nation, under God, shall have a new birth of freedom – and that government of the people, by the people, for the people, shall not perish from the earth.

Recognizing that the nation was founded on the First Principles of free and just government, Lincoln's short but magnificent speech characterized the nation as a Social Compact based on the equality of all men and established to protect liberty. The power of the *Gettysburg Address*, much like the power of Douglass' and Garnet's speeches, was the recognition of America's unfulfilled promise of equality. The Address also harkens back to the Lockean-Hobbesian dilemma. Only by recognizing the inherent worth of each individual and the purpose of government as the protection of unalienable rights could slavery be abolished; and only by denying the inherent worth of each individual and unalienable rights of men could slavery exist. The Address became a linchpin in the development of the American character by transforming a war for Union into a war for equality.

The words were soon put into action. In January, 1865, the country ratified the Thirteenth Amendment of the Constitution and abolished slavery and involuntary servitude (except as punishment for a crime). America had taken momentous strides to fulfilling the promise of its First Principle of equality.

RECONSTRUCTION

Many of the framers and ratifiers of the Thirteenth Amendment assumed that with the abolition of slavery that African Americans would begin to gain their equal rights. They were mistaken. The freedmen were not liberated from the animus of slavery and racism. Despite their courageous service during the Civil War – they fought in over four hundred battles – the nation did little when Southern states enacted Black Codes that infringed upon African Americans' rights to bear arms, free speech, assembly, marriage (to whites), and other vital liberties.[259] These laws often restricted African Americans' economic liberty and mandated harsh and unjust terms of employment for farmers, including forced labor and forfeiture of prior earnings, in direct contradiction of centuries of contract law. The regulation of labor contracts was simply a subterfuge to force freedmen back into the hands of the plantation owners and to deprive them of their civil liberties.

Congress – dominated by Republicans (often referred to as "Radical Republicans") strongly committed to the cause of equality and the use of federal power to protect the rights of freedmen – reacted quickly. The *Freedmen's Bureau Act* (1865) would have authorized federal troops to manage and supervise abandoned property, as well as provide provisions, clothing, fuel, and shelter for freedmen and refugees. The act also would have set aside up to forty acres of land for every male citizen freedman or refugee. The recipients would have been protected in the use and enjoyment of the land for three years at a fixed annual rent, with the option to purchase at the end of the term. President Andrew Johnson vetoed the measure – and the attempt to override the veto fell two votes short in the Senate.

Johnson had been catapulted to the presidency upon Lincoln's assassination in April, 1865 by the Confederate sympathizer John Wilkes Booth. Lincoln, the Great Emancipator, was murdered because of his courageous service toward saving the Union. A giant of America, his successor would be severely tested. A Tennessee Democrat, Johnson wished to quickly reunify the nation on very lenient terms. Like Lincoln, he had humble beginnings, but was much better at winning elections than Lincoln ever was. Beginning in 1829, Johnson held office almost successively – he served as an alderman, state legislator, congressman, Governor, and United States Senator. When he first took the office of President, he stated that "treason is a crime, and crime must be punished," but offered a meager plan for Reconstruction. Soon he opposed all but the most modest attempts to secure the liberty and equality of the freedmen.

The Radical Republican Congress, however, would not be denied. Led by Senator Charles Sumner and Representative Thaddeus Stevens, the Radical Republicans won a resounding victory in the midterm elections of 1866, repudiating President Johnson's opposition to ensuring political equality of the freedman through the federal government. Sumner had been previously rewarded for his intense, passionate leadership on behalf of abolitionism and civil equality by being beat senseless in 1856 as he sat at his Senate chair by Representative Preston S. Brooks of South Carolina. Sumner, who never quite recovered from the assault, attacked the "demon of Caste" based on race and proclaimed that "The same national authority that destroyed slavery must see that this other pretension is not permitted to survive."[260] He helped lead the effort to pass the *Civil Rights Act of 1866* over Johnson's veto.

The act provided that all persons "of every race and color, without regard to any previous condition of slavery or involuntary servitude" born in the United States were citizens of the country. The first major piece of legislation passed over a President's veto, Section 1 of the act ensured that each citizen possesses "the same right . . . to make and enforce contracts, to sue, be parties, and give evidence, to inherit, purchase, lease, sell, hold, and convey real and personal property, as is enjoyed by white citizens, and shall be subject to like punishment, pains, and penalties, and to no other." Congress also passed the *First Reconstruction Act* (1867) over President Johnson's veto, which placed a duty on the occupying federal troops in the South "to protect all persons in their rights of persons and property, to suppress insurrection, disorder, and violence."

Lingering doubts regarding the constitutionality of the *Civil Rights Act of 1866* induced the passage of the Fourteenth Amendment to the Constitution in 1868. This Amendment prohibits states from depriving "any person within its jurisdiction equal protection of the laws," and prevents any state from depriving "any person of life, liberty, or property without due process of law." The Amendment also guarantees that all persons born or naturalized in the United States are American citizens and prohibits states from abridging "the privileges and immunities of citizens of the United States."

The Fourteenth Amendment reversed the historical understanding of liberty in the United States. Until its passage, states were understood to be the great guarantors of individual liberty. Radical Republicans, however, understood that many states would continue to deny African Americans individual rights and equality before the law unless the Constitution prohibited such discrimination. Section 5 of the Fourteenth Amendment grants Congress the power to legislate to maintain the integrity of the Amendment, thereby placing the protection of equality and some rights from state tyranny in the hands of Congress. The Amendment, in other words, bars oppressive governmental action from state governments, thereby supplementing the Bill of Rights, which had been directed almost exclusively at the federal government. Similarly, the Fifteenth Amendment, ratified in 1870, guarantees the right to vote regardless of race and authorizes Congress to legislate to protect the franchise.

Such measures provoked heated opposition from the South and President Johnson. Congress, however, was not to be stymied in its pursuit of political equality for all races. In fact, Johnson's intransigence brought about the first impeachment of a President. The *Articles of Impeachment* (1868) adopted by the House of Representatives charged that Johnson had, among other things, attacked the Congress and attempted to prevent enforcement of the four Reconstruction Acts. The House impeached Johnson, but the Senate refused to convict – by one vote. Nevertheless, the Radical Republican Congress was victorious in implementing most of its agenda.

Newly emboldened, and with the Civil War hero General Ulysses S. Grant elected President in 1868, Congress passed the *Force Acts* in 1870, which imposed heavy penalties for violations of the Fourteenth and Fifteenth Amendments. Meanwhile, Southern resistance to Reconstruction spawned the Klu Klux Klan. The Klan terrorized freedmen and undermined federal efforts to ensure equality. In response, the *Enforcement Act (Klu Klux Klan Act) of 1871* placed congressional elections under federal control, and authorized the filing of civil lawsuits against government employees acting under the color of law who deprived persons of any rights, privileges, or immunities secured by the Constitution. The *Enforcement Act* also criminalized conspiracy to delay the execution of the law, threats against federal officials performing federal law, and protected witnesses and jurors of federal courts. Moreover, the act also defended the equal protection of the laws from force, intimidation, or threat; and protected the right to vote and free speech with regard to federal elections. Recognizing that racial discrimination was still pervasive in the South, the *Civil Rights Act of 1875* went so far as to mandate that "all persons . . . be entitled to the full and equal enjoyment of the accommodations, advantages, facilities, and privileges of inns, public conveyances on land or water, theaters, and other places of public amusement."

With the aid of federal troops, the Reconstruction Amendments, and civil rights acts, African Americans were able to register to vote and exercise the franchise in the South for the first time in American history. With Reconstruction being enforced by federal troops in the South, African Americans were consistently elected to state legislatures and Congress. Missouri, for example, was represented by two African American Senators. African Americans were able to participate in the formation of new state constitutions and even dominated the South Carolina legislature for two years.

The Civil War Amendments and Reconstruction acts were large and magnificent steps in the march toward equality. While experiencing many difficulties, Reconstruction brought forward a strong federal commitment to fulfill the promise of equality.

JIM CROW

The promise of Reconstruction, however, would regrettably be lost in 1876 and not regained until almost a century later. The federal government and the general public grew weary of Reconstruction and the sharp divisions it wrought. Reconstruction not only continued the North-South division of the nation, it created additional fractures – federal policy had created divisions between the Radical Republicans and moderates who opposed vigorous enforcement of civil rights laws. The country had been consumed by the race issue for decades; hundreds of thousands of men had been sacrificed in the Civil War; and an army of occupation was required to enforce Reconstruction.

In this context the election of 1876 took place between moderate Republican candidate Governor Rutherford B. Hayes of Ohio and Democratic candidate Governor Samuel J. Tilden of New York. The electoral votes of four states were hotly disputed leaving Tilden one electoral vote shy of election. After a contentious, likely corrupt, and tortuous months-long process over disputed electoral votes, Hayes was elected the President by the House of Representatives. Many historians have concluded that Hayes (or Republicans in Congress) expressly or implicitly promised to remove the remaining federal troops in the South in exchange for the House of Representatives' declaration that he won the election. In any event, he removed those troops within a month after taking office.

With the end of federal occupation of the South also came the end of Reconstruction. Soon "Jim Crow" laws resulted in the segregation and political disenfranchisement of African Americans in the South. The overwhelmingly illiterate and poor African American population was kept from the ballot box by unfairly applied literacy tests, severe poll taxes, tissue ballots, and other affronts to the suffrage. White supremacists began rampages of terror – cross burnings, arson, and lynchings became all too commonplace. Segregation by race became the law and practice of the land. The dismal results on African American life were described by Frederick Douglass in 1883:

> Flagrant as have been the outrages committed upon colored citizens in respect to the civil rights, more flagrant, shocking and scandalous still have been the outrages committed upon our political rights, by means of bull-dozing and Klukluxing, Mississippi plans, fraudulent counts, tissue ballots and the like devices. Three states in which the colored people outnumber the white population are without colored representation and their political voice suppressed. The colored citizens in those States are virtually disenfranchised, the Constitution held in utter contempt and its provisions nullified.[261]

All the emancipated slaves asked for, Douglass explained, was simply "an equal chance in the race of life,"[262] to be given "fair play, and let him alone."[263] The *Civil Rights Acts* of 1866 and 1875 had been enacted to do just that. By prohibiting discrimination based on race, the Radical Republican Congress intended to create a more level playing field in which African Americans and whites would both be able to participate in life on an equal footing. With the withdrawal of federal troops from the South, however, there was no power to enforce those acts – save the courts.

The courts, however, forsook their duties. The United States Supreme Court – presumably the great guardian of individual rights – began to gut the Reconstruction Amendments even before the federal troops had left the South. In the appropriately named *Slaughterhouse Cases* (1872),[264] the Court eviscerated the Privileges and Immunities Clause of the Fourteenth Amendment. Representative John Bingham of Ohio, drafter of the clause, and Senator Jacob Howard of Michigan, sponsor of the Amendment in the Senate, stated that the Privileges and Immunities Clause was intended to apply the protections of the Bill of Rights (which applied almost exclusively against the federal government) against the state governments.

The Court, however, found that the Fourteenth Amendment only prohibited states from infringing on the rights of "American citizenship." The potentially powerful clause was reduced to protecting such liberties as the right to travel on the high seas and between the states, while ignoring other core liberties as free speech, due process, and free exercise of religion. The Court found that it would not broadly interpret the clause because such an interpretation "radically changes the whole theory of relations between the state and Federal governments to each other and of both these governments to the people."[265] The Court, of course, ignored the obvious conclusion that such a "radical" change was the very purpose of the Amendment framed and ratified by the Radical Republicans in the wake of the Civil War, the emancipation of the slaves, and the enactment of several groundbreaking civil rights acts.

The Court also struck down the rarely enforced *Civil Rights Act of 1875*. In *The Civil Rights Cases* (1883),[266] the Court found that neither the Thirteenth nor Fourteenth Amendments granted Congress the power to prohibit private discrimination. Justice John Marshall Harlan, a former slave owner and opponent of the Reconstruction Amendments, was the sole dissenter. Relying upon the circumstances and history surrounding the adoption of the Thirteenth Amendment, he found that it provided Congress with the power to eliminate the "badges and incidents" of slavery. Congress, therefore, could adopt Civil Rights legislation, including the authority to bar racial discrimination in public.[267] Harlan also found that the power granted by the Fourteenth Amendment to Congress authorized civil rights legislation.

Despite the intention of the ratifiers of the Reconstruction Amendments, the Southern states were determined to maintain as many of the badges and incidents of slavery as possible. Emboldened by *The Civil Rights Cases*, the South became riddled with segregationist laws mandating the separation of the races in a variety of contexts. While slavery had been abolished, the Southern states refused to recognize the equality of all races and subjected African Americans to humiliating segregation – a constant reminder of their former status as chattel.

The Supreme Court, in the infamous case of *Plessy v Ferguson* (1896),[268] upheld the constitutionality of such laws. In *Plessy*, the plaintiffs challenged a law in Louisiana requiring "separate but equal" accommodations for African Americans and whites on railroads. Justice Harlan, again dissenting, found that the law violated the fundamental purpose of the Reconstruction Amendments. Those Amendments, he found, "were welcomed by the friends of liberty throughout the world. They removed the race line from our governments."[269] Laws mandating segregation by race, Harlan explained, were a clever subterfuge "under the guise of giving equal accommodation for whites and blacks, to compel the latter to keep to themselves. . . ."[270] More important, Harlan found, the Reconstruction Amendments mandated equality before the law, and segregation laws struck at the heart of those Amendments:

> [I]n view of the constitution, in the eye of the law, there is in this country no superior, dominant, ruling class of citizens. There is no caste here. Our constitution is color-blind, and neither knows nor tolerates classes among citizens. In respect of civil rights, all citizens are equal before the law. The humblest is the peer to the most powerful. The law regards man as man, and takes no account of his surroundings or of his color when his civil rights as guaranteed by the supreme law are involved. . . .
>
> The arbitrary separation of citizens, on the basis of race, while they are on a public highway, is a badge of servitude wholly inconsistent with the civil freedom and the equality before the law established by the constitution. It cannot be justified upon any legal grounds.[271]

Harlan's reasoning not only comported with the plain meaning of the Amendment, it also matched the original understanding of the authors of the constitutional provision when it was adopted. Senator Lyman Trumbull, Chair of the Senate Judiciary Committee that reported the Thirteenth Amendment, explained during the ratification debate in Congress that "any statute which is not equal to all, and which deprives any citizen of civil rights, which are secured to other citizens, is an unjust encroachment upon his liberty; and it is in fact a badge of servitude which by the Constitution is prohibited."[272]

The majority of the Court, however, upheld the Louisiana law. The Court reasoned that "A statute which implies merely a legal distinction between the white and colored races – a distinction which is founded in the color of the two races, and which always must exist so long as white men are distinguished from the other race by color – has no tendency to destroy the legal equality of the two races, or re-establish a state of involuntary servitude."[273] This, perhaps, was the Court's most loathsome opinion.

Although the nation had ratified the Reconstruction Amendments and the Radical Republican Congress had enacted a series of strong civil rights laws, equality before the law was more of an aspiration than a reality. With the federal government's withdrawal of troops from the South and the Supreme Court's refusal to enforce the Constitution or the Reconstruction Acts, the promise of equality was broken. Jim Crow had not only swept through the South, he occupied the White House and the Supreme Court. John Hope, in his *Reply to Brooker T. Washington* in 1896, cut to the chase: "If we cannot do what other freemen do, then we are not free."

THE RENEWED CIVIL RIGHTS STRUGGLE

Generations after the *Emancipation Proclamation*, Dr Martin Luther King, Jr explained the state of America:

> But one hundred years later, we must face the tragic fact
> that the Negro is still not free. One hundred years later, the
> life of the Negro is still sadly crippled by the manacles of

segregation and the chains of discrimination. One hundred years later, the Negro lives on a lonely island of poverty in the midst of a vast ocean of material prosperity. One hundred years later, the Negro is still languished in the corners of American society and finds himself an exile in his own land. . . .

When the architects of our republic wrote the magnificent words of the Constitution and the *Declaration of Independence*, they were signing a promissory note to which every American was to fall heir. This note was a promise that all men would be guaranteed the unalienable rights of life, liberty, and the pursuit of happiness.

It is obvious today that America has defaulted on this promissory note insofar as her citizens of color are concerned.[274]

Indeed, not until the Civil Rights Movement of the 1950s and 1960s did African Americans begin to gain the equality under law promised to them almost a century before. In 1954, the United States Supreme Court, led by Chief Justice Earl Warren, reversed itself and began to revive the Reconstruction Amendments. In *Brown v Topeka Board of Education*,[275] the Court struck down state segregated public schools. Warren, a former Republican Governor of California and vice-presidential candidate, authored the opinion overturning *Plessy v Ferguson* and the legacy of "separate but equal." Under his leadership the Court ruled that "in the field of public education the doctrine of 'separate but equal' has no place. Separate educational facilities are inherently unequal."[276]

Civil unrest and street confrontations between white segregationists and civil rights supporters followed the decision. Led by the National Association for the Advancement of Colored People (NAACP), civil rights leaders attempted to implement the *Brown* decision by integrating the public schools. Not until 1957 was the Court's ruling definitively enforced by President Dwight Eisenhower's ordering of federal troops and national guardsmen to enforce the integration of Central High School in Little Rock, Arkansas.

Federal troops had once again returned to the South to protect the equality of African Americans.

In Alabama, Rosa Parks sparked the famous Montgomery Bus Boycott. Parks defied Southern segregationist laws by simply refusing to sit in the back of the bus. The boycott, from 1955-1956, began a series of protest actions by African Americans and civil rights supporters across the South. Economic boycotts, sit-ins, marches, freedom rides, and other protest techniques pushed the South – and the whole nation – to again confront the issue of equality.

The results were long overdue and remarkable. In 1956, the Supreme Court struck down segregated seating on buses, and in 1957 Congress passed a *Civil Rights Act* establishing the Civil Rights division of the Department of Justice and authorizing the division to seek injunctions against voting rights violations. The *Civil Rights Act of 1960* authorized strong federal enforcement of the 1957 Act. In 1961 the Interstate Commerce Commission prohibited segregation on buses and terminals in interstate commerce, and railroad and airlines followed suit voluntarily. The same year, President John F. Kennedy issued an executive order creating the Commission on Equal Employment Opportunity, which was designed to root out discrimination in employment.

The beginning of desegregation of public universities became reality when African Americans, led by James Meredith at the University of Mississippi in September, 1962, broke the white monopoly of attendance in the major universities in the South. The ratification of the Twenty-Fourth Amendment in 1964 prohibited poll taxes for federal elections – eliminating a major barrier to the ballot box for minorities. The *Civil Rights Act of 1964* increased voting protection, prohibited discrimination in areas of public accommodation, withdrew federal money from state or local programs that discriminated, empowered the Attorney General to institute law suits to desegregate schools, and established the Equal Employment Opportunity Commission to forbid discriminatory employment practices.

The constitutionality of the act was upheld in 1964 by the United States Supreme Court in *Heart of Atlanta Motel v United States*[277] and *Katzenbach v McClung*.[278] The *Voting Rights Act of 1965* enforced the Fifteenth and Twenty-Fourth Amendments by banning literacy tests, empowering federal examiners to ensure the integrity of the voting process, and authorizing the Attorney General to institute suits against the use of poll taxes. The United States Supreme Court soon struck down laws prohibiting cohabitation of different races[279] as well as those barring interracial marriage[280] as violations of the Equal Protection Clause of the Fourteenth Amendment. Payments towards the promissory note were finally forthcoming.

The impetus underlying the Civil Rights Movement, like the drive to abolish slavery and to enact the Reconstruction Amendments, was the belief in the First Principle that all persons, regardless of race or heritage, are equal before the law. The Reverend Martin Luther King, Jr, the greatest leader of the Civil Rights Movement, firmly believed in this conviction and used it as his greatest weapon. King, who preached and practiced non-violent opposition in the face of oppression, established the Southern Christian Leadership Conference in 1957, and led the struggle for equality during the Montgomery Bus Boycott. Awarded the Nobel Peace Prize in 1964 for his leadership across the South in fighting for racial justice, he would be assassinated in Memphis, Tennessee four years later.

Writing from a jail cell in Birmingham, Alabama in 1963, he predicted that African Americans "will reach the goal of freedom in Birmingham and all over the nation, because the goal of America is freedom." He explained that "One day the South will know that when these disinherited children of God sat down at lunch counters, they were in reality standing up for what is best in the American dream and for the sacred values in our Judaeo-Christian heritage, thereby bringing our nation back to those great wells of democracy which were dug deep by the founding fathers in their formulation of the Constitution and the *Declaration of Independence*."[281] Thus, it was natural for King, when he addressed over 200,000 supporters who had marched on Washington, D.C. in support of a civil rights bill, to echo Jefferson, Lincoln, Douglass, and Harlan:

I have a dream. It is rooted deeply in the American dream.

I have a dream that one day this nation will rise up and live out the true meaning of its creed: "We hold these truths to be self-evident; that all men are created equal."

I have a dream that one day on the red hills of Georgia the sons of former slaves and the sons of former slaveowners will be able to sit down together at the table of brother-hood. . . .

I have a dream that my four little children will one day live in a nation where they will not be judged by the color of their skin but by the content of their character.[282]

While such a vision was once fantasy, the major advances in civil rights in the 1950s and 1960s moved the nation closer to the reality of equality under the law. Slow and hard was the progress, but it continued thereafter. In November, 1995, former head of the National Security Council and Chief of the Joint Chiefs of Staff (and future Secretary of State) Colin Powell reflected on his personal, and his generation's, remarkable progress:

In our generation we have moved from denying a black man service at the lunch counter to elevating one to the highest military office in the nation, and to being a serious contender for the presidency.

This is a magnificent country and I am proud to be one of its sons.

At the time of the Revolution and the forming of the Constitution equality had been largely limited to whites, but the First Principle of equality powerfully worked a subsequent revolution: the equality of all races. Animated by the First Principles of free and just government, America abolished slavery, amended the Constitution to provide for the equal protection of the laws, extended the franchise to all races, and embodied civil rights into its laws. While there is no doubt that Dr King's dream is not yet reality, inspired by the First Principle of equality, the nation is dedicated to its fulfillment.

Chapter 8
Embracing Gender Equality

But when a long train of abuses and usurpations, pursuing invariably the same object, evinces a design to reduce them under absolute despotism, it is their duty to throw off such government, and to provide new guards for their future security. Such has been the patient sufferance of the women under this government, and such is now the necessity which constrains them to demand the equal station to which they are entitled. Elizabeth Cady Stanton, *Seneca Falls Declaration of Sentiments and Resolutions* (1848).

❈   For the Founding Fathers, equality, the Social Compact, and recognition and protection of unalienable rights had been mostly limited to men, but animated by the First Principles, America enfranchised women and enacted supportive civil rights legislation

❈   Although the struggle for gender equality is incomplete, inspired by our First Principles, the nation is dedicated to its fulfillment

---

The inclusion of all races into the American polity did not ensure that all Americans would be treated as equal citizens. Women were still excluded from the First Principles of free and just government. From the Revolution until the early twentieth century, no women possessed substantial political rights, and married women possessed no substantial economic rights. That gender inequality could exist in a land founded on the First Principles of equality, protection of unalienable rights, and the Social Compact presented an inevitable conflict. Fortunately, a civil war was not needed to extend the blessings of American liberty to women, but it would take a momentous struggle culminating in the ratification of the Nineteenth Amendment. Many more decades would pass, however, before women would approach true equality under the law. Even now, America is not entirely free from its legacy of gender inequality.

Not unlike the struggle for racial equality, the struggle for gender equality has a long and complex history that is beyond the scope of this work. The purpose of this Chapter is to explore how the basic contradiction between our First Principles and gender inequality resulted in the movement for gender equality.

Gender Oppression in the Land of Equality

At the time of the American Revolution, the few women who argued for equality were simply ignored. Abigail Adams – the witty and insightful wife of John Adams – wrote that men were "Naturally Tyrannical is a Truth so thoroughly established as to admit of no dispute. . . . Men of Sense of all Ages abhor those customs which treat us only as the vassals of your Sex."[283] When, on the eve of the Revolution, she drafted an outline for the codification of gender equality, her husband's answer was dismissive:

> As to your extraordinary Code of Laws, I cannot but laugh. We have been told that our Struggle has loosened the bands of Government every where. . . . But your Letter was the first Intimation that another tribe more numerous and powerful than all the rest were grown discontented. . . .
>
> Depend upon it, we know better than to repeal our Masculine systems. . . . We dare not exert our Power in its full Latitude. We are obliged to go fair, and softly, and in Practice you know that We are the subjects.[284]

Despite John Adams' protests to the contrary, seventy years later, Elizabeth Cady Stanton could comprehensively outline the inequitable treatment of women:

> The history of mankind is a history of repeated injuries and usurpations on the part of man toward woman, having in direct object the establishment of an absolute tyranny over her. To prove this, let facts be submitted to a candid world.
>
> He has never permitted her to exercise her inalienable right to the elective franchise.
>
> He has compelled her to submit to laws, in the formation of which she had no voice.
>
> He has withheld from her rights which are given to the most ignorant and degraded men – both natives and foreigners. . . .
>
> He has made her, if married, in the eye of the law, civilly dead.
>
> He has taken from her all right in property, even to the wages she earns. . . .
>
> He has monopolized nearly all the profitable employments, and from those she is permitted to follow, she receives but a scanty remuneration.
>
> He closes against her all avenues to wealth and distinction, which he considers most honorable to himself. As a teacher of theology, medicine, or law, she is not known. . . .[285]

Although not in bondage, "The wife who inherits no property holds about the same legal position that does the slave of the Southern plantation," Stanton, a leading suffragette, could accurately remark before the New

York State Legislature in 1854. The first woman ever to address that body, Stanton continued: "She can own nothing, sell nothing. She has no right even to the wages she earns; her person, her time, her services are the property of another." As Sarah M. Grimke wrote in an insightful letter in 1837, "Woman, instead of being elevated by her union with man, which might be expected from an alliance with a superior being, is in reality lowered. She generally loses her individuality, her independent character, her moral being. She becomes absorbed into him, and henceforth is looked at, and acts through the medium of her husband."[286]

The political establishment believed that women were incapable of performing the basic tasks necessary for participation in politics, business, science, and the arts. The political patriarchy did not consider women able to possess the correct temperament, stamina, or talents to be full participants in the American experiment. Justice Joseph Bradley of the United States Supreme Court, in a concurring opinion upholding the Illinois Bar's prohibition of women from the practice of law, epitomized these sentiments:

> [T]he civil law, as well as nature herself, has recognized a wide difference in the respective spheres and destinies of man and woman. Man is, or should be, woman's protector and defender. The natural timidity and delicacy which belongs to the female sex evidently unfits it for many occupations of civil life.[287]

Grimke explained that this so called protective status made women "among the lowest classes of society," and ironically ensured that many women would "suffer intensely from the brutality of their husbands." Instead of elevating women, their second-class status harshly subjected many to "Brute force" and "the law of violence," thereby making such women little more than the drudges of men.[288] Grimke, the daughter of a prominent Charleston, South Carolina slave-holding family, traveled on a speaking tour with her sister Angelina to New England and New York in the 1830s to attack slavery. When criticized by clergymen for publicly speaking out against that peculiar institution, Grimke and her sister realized that like African Americans, women were not afforded equality. Indeed, Grimke observed that her experience showed that men had "done all he could to debase and enslave her mind. . . ."[289]

Stanton convincingly explained many of the parallels between slaves and women in ante-bellum America:

> The negro has no name. He is Cuffy Douglas or Cuffy Brookes, just whose Cuffy he may chance to be. The woman has no name. She is Mrs. Richard Roe or Mrs. John Doe, just whose Mrs. she may chance to be. Cuffy has no right to his earnings; he can not buy or sell, or lay up anything that he can call his own. Cuffy has no right to his children; they can be sold from him at any time. Mrs. Roe has no right to her children; they may be bound out to cancel a father's debts of honor. The unborn child, even, by the last will of the father, may be placed under the guardianship of a stranger or a foreigner. Cuffy has no legal existence; he is subject to restraint and moderate chastisement. Mrs. Roe has no legal existence; she has not the best right to her own person. The husband has the power to restrain, and administer moderate chastisement.[290]

In short, even after the Revolution and the adoption of the Constitution, "The negro's skin and the woman's sex are both *prima facie* evidence that they were intended to be in subjection to the white Saxon man."[291] Women were not afforded the protections of the First Principles of free and just government. "For [women] this government is not a democracy; it is not a republic," remarked Susan B. Anthony, "It is the most odious aristocracy ever established on the face of the globe."[292]

Women trapped in brutal marriages were not protected by the law; the law protected only a few of a woman's unalienable rights; equality – political, economic, and social – was unattainable; women were excluded from the Social Compact; and the end of government was not to protect women, but to subject them to the rule of men. Like racial minorities, at its founding and generations thereafter the promise of America was not offered to women.

The Movement for Gender Equality

Like African Americans, women understood the hypocrisy of their situation. While the American Revolution had been fought for liberty based upon the equality of individuals, they were denied such equality. Not unlike slaves and freedmen, women would begin to fight for their liberty and equality by harkening to the First Principles by which the Revolution and Constitution were forged.

Because of its unique government based on the promise of equality, the United States became the world center of feminism. The first significant organized movement for women's equality began in America in 1848 – and it claimed the principles of 1776 and 1789 as its own. Eight years earlier, Stanton met Lucretia Mott, a Quaker minister, at the World Anti-Slavery Convention in London. Energized by the convention's refusal to allow women to openly participate in the proceedings (women were required to sit behind a curtain), Stanton and Mott resolved to hold a woman's rights conference in America. Belatedly held in Seneca Falls, New York in 1848, the conference participants vigorously attacked the disenfranchisement of women and their unequal treatment as violative of the First Principles of free and just government. In fact, the *Declaration of Sentiments and Resolutions* issued from the conference parallels the *Declaration of Independence*:

> We hold these truths to be self-evident; that all men and women are created equal, that they are endowed by their Creator with certain inalienable rights; that among these are life, liberty, and the pursuit of happiness; that to secure these rights governments are instituted, deriving their just powers from the consent of the governed.

Throughout her long career as a vital leader of the suffrage movement, Susan B. Anthony similarly evoked America's First Principles. She asked, for example, "how can 'the consent of the governed' be given, if the right to vote be denied?" In fact, women lived under the rule of a government that "enforces taxation without representation – that compels them to obey laws to which they never have given their consent – that imprisons and hangs them without a trial by a jury of their peers – that robs them, in marriage, of the custody of their own persons, wages, and children – are this half of the people who are left wholly at the mercy of the other half, in direct violation of the spirit and the letter of the declarations of the framers of this government, every one of which was based on the immutable principle of equal rights to all."[293]

Anthony recognized the heart of the matter: governance without consent. The cause that triggered the American Revolution was denied to half of Americans based solely on gender. As she succinctly stated, "It is downright mockery to talk to women of their enjoyment of the blessings of liberty while they are denied the only means of securing them provided by this democratic-republican government – the ballot."[294]

Soon after Seneca Falls, Stanton and Anthony became partners in a fruitful, if not tumultuous, relationship that would culminate in women's suffrage decades later. They were peculiar partners. Stanton was full-time mother and housekeeper. She was also married to a politician who little understood her egalitarian beliefs. Anthony, single and childless, was an effective and tireless organizer for the movement, while Stanton was a powerful writer and orator.

During their many years of collaboration, Stanton and Anthony overcame many pitfalls. The passage of the Fourteenth Amendment, for example, was paradoxically a great victory and a great loss for their movement. The drafters of the Amendment purposefully omitted gender from the express language of the Equal Protection Clause. On the other hand, the plain language of the Amendment appeared to grant all "persons" – including women – equal protection of the laws. While bitterly disappointed by the Amendment's omission of gender equality, the suffragists used it as sharp, new weapon to agitate for equal rights. Anthony recalled that when she approached Senator Sumner "to declare the power of the United States Constitution to protect women in their right to vote – as he had done for black men – he handed me a copy of all his speeches during that reconstruction period, and said: 'Put "sex" where I have "race" or "color," and you have here the best and strongest argument I can make for woman.'"[295]

Anthony followed Sumner's advice – as did the rest of the movement. Anthony, however, also went a step further and argued that "the adoption of the Fourteenth Amendment settled the question forever in its first sentence. .

. . The second settles the equal status of all citizens. . . . The only question left to be settled now is: Are women persons?"[296] Stanton likewise argued that "if we consider her as citizen . . . she must have the same rights as all other members, according to the fundamental principles of our government."[297]

First targeting states, and then a new federal constitutional amendment, the success of the suffrage movement hinged upon convincing men that women were entitled to basic political rights and capable of exercising such rights. Contrary to the beliefs of many men (and women), Stanton argued that women could competently exercise such rights:

> We have every qualification required by the Constitution, necessary to the legal voter, but the one of sex. We are moral, virtuous, and intelligent, and in all respects quite equal to the proud white man himself. . . . [W]e, who have guided great movements of charity, established missions, edited journals, published works on history, economy, and statistics; who have governed nations, led armies, filled the professor's chair, taught philosophy and mathematics to the savants of our age, discovered planets, piloted ships across the sea, are denied the most sacred rights of citizens, because, forsooth, we came not into this republic crowned with the dignity of manhood![298]

Eschewing the special legal protections and barriers that the law had placed on and in the way of women because of their gender, the suffrage movement demanded only that women be treated as equals before the law: "we ask for all that you have asked for yourselves . . . and simply on the ground that the rights of every human being are the same and identical."[299] Stanton, therefore, decried special legislation that in the name of protecting women deprived them of equal protection of the law:

> But if, gentlemen, you take the ground that sexes are alike, and, therefore, you are our faithful representatives – then why all the special laws for woman? Would not one code answer for all of like needs and wants? Christ's golden rule is better than all the special legislation that the ingenuity of

man can devise: 'Do unto others as you would have others do unto you.' This, men and brethren, is all we ask at your hands. We ask no better laws than those you have made for yourselves. We need no other protection than that which your present laws secure to you.[300]

Speaking for the suffrage movement, Stanton rejected the necessity of special legislation, noting that "Nothing strengthens the judgment and quickens the conscience like individual responsibility. Nothing adds such dignity to character as the recognition of one's self-sovereignty; the right to an equal place, everywhere conceded – a place earned by personal merit, not an artificial attainment by inheritance, wealth, family and position."[301] In fact, "The talk of sheltering woman from the fierce storms of life is the sheerest mockery," she wrote, "for they beat on her from every point on the compass, just as they do on man, and with more fatal results, for he has been trained to protect himself, to resist, and to conquer."[302] In truth, she continued, women "as a class, are tired of one kind of protection, that which leaves us everything to do, to dare, and to suffer, and strips us of all means for its accomplishment."[303] Thus, in her *Address to the New York Legislature* in 1860, she demanded the elimination of all gender-based legislation:

Undo what man did for us in the dark ages, and strike out all special legislation for us; strike the words "white male" from all your constitutions, and then, with fair sailing, let us sink or swim, live or die, survive or perish together.

Grimke wrote similarly that "I ask no favors for my sex. I surrender not our claim to equality. All I ask of our brethren is, that they will take their feet from off our necks and permit us to stand upright on that ground which God designed us to occupy."[304]

Armed with America's First Principles and opposing special protection, the woman's movement assaulted the American patriarchy.

SUFFRAGE AND BEYOND

Like the struggle for racial equality, the campaign for gender equality was slow to achieve success. The First Principles of equality, the Social Compact, and the recognition and protection of unalienable rights eroded bit-by-bit the patriarchal nature of the law and much of society. New York's *Married Women's Property Act of 1848* broke new ground. Followed in other states, the act granted a woman control over her personal property, even after marriage. The passage of the act was strongly influenced by a novel petition drive – organized by and for women regarding a women's issue. New York set the trend again by enacting the *Married Women's Property Act of 1860* one month after Stanton addressed the legislature. The act guaranteed women the rights to work, contract, to sue and be sued, to carry on a business or enterprise, and to keep their own earnings. The act also granted women equal powers with their husbands as joint guardians of their children, and equal rights of inheritance regardless of which spouse died first. Building on these and other early successes, after a long and arduous campaign based on the First Principles, on August 26, 1920 the nation ratified the Nineteenth Amendment to the Constitution, which guaranteed women the franchise.

Despite such impressive gains, women remained in the background of American politics, culture, economics, and society for decades. Prevailing social attitudes generally locked women into the home and out of factories, professions, sciences, and the arts.

Persuaded by Esther Peterson, the head of the Women's Bureau of the Department of Labor, President Kennedy appointed a Presidential Commission on the Status of Women and tapped Eleanor Roosevelt as its chair. The final report documented pervasive employment discrimination against women regarding job opportunities, pay, and other key aspects of employment. Kennedy responded by requiring the federal civil service to hire without regard to gender. The *Equal Pay Act of 1963* prohibited unequal pay for equal work.

The *Civil Rights Act of 1964* was another tremendous step towards gender equality by prohibiting employment discrimination based on gender. Similar protections were enacted in state constitutions and laws. The federal Equal Employment and Opportunity Commission (EEOC) was established under the *Civil Rights Act of 1964*, and began to attack gender discrimination. Passed in the early 1970s, the *Equal Opportunity Act* broadened the jurisdiction and enforcement capabilities of the EEOC. A long neglected fact of life for far too many women, sexual harassment in the workplace, on campus, and elsewhere came under intense scrutiny and remediation in the 1980s and 1990s by the EEOC, civil rights organizations, and the courts.

Furthermore, the Supreme Court found that government sponsored gender discrimination violates the Equal Protection Clause of the Fourteenth Amendment if it does not serve an important governmental interest and gender discrimination is not substantially related to such interests.[305] While not as rigorous as the scrutiny applied to racial classifications, this standard substantially protects women and men from unjust governmental discrimination based on gender.

After years of struggle, many women have gained the opportunity to participate – and win – in the market, arts, sciences, academia, and politics. Record numbers of women hold quality jobs in the workplace, hold political office, and contribute to science and culture. Women are leaders and excelling in politics, law, medicine, the arts, business, science, academics, literature, sports, and other fields. Supreme Court Justice Sandra Day O'Connor, appointed by President Reagan, was the pivotal swing vote on the Supreme Court for two decades. Women have served in several cabinet positions under President Bill Clinton and President George W. Bush, including the leading position of Secretary of State (indeed, Bush's Secretary of State Condoleezza Rice is an African American woman). A woman has ascended to the Speaker of the House. Women have been and continue to be serious contenders for the presidency.

Using the First Principles of free and just government, America became dedicated to the ideal of gender equality and secured women the franchise, abolished civil disabilities applicable to women, and guaranteed women equal protection of the laws and civil rights. Much like racial equality, however, the work of achieving gender equality and fully integrating women into society on the basis of our First Principles has been – and continues to be – an aspiration.

PART III
RECLAIMING AMERICA'S
FIRST PRINCIPLES AND HISTORY

Had the people of the United States been educated in different principles, had they been less intelligent, less independent, or less virtuous, can it be believed that we would have maintained the same steady and consistent career or been blessed with the same success? While, then, the constituent body retains its present and sound and healthy state everything will be safe. . . . It is only when the people become ignorant and corrupt, when they degenerate into a populace, that they are incapable of exercising sovereignty. Usurpation is then an easy attainment, and an usurper soon found. The people themselves become the willing instruments of their own debasement and ruin. Let us, then, look to the great cause, and endeavor to preserve it in full force. Let us by all wise and constitutional measures promote intelligence among the people as the best means of preserving our liberties. James Monroe, *First Inaugural Address* (1817).

Chapter 9
Education, Legal, Holiday, Media, Nonprofit, and Political Reform

[A] frequent recurrence to the fundamental principles is absolutely necessary, to preserve the blessings of liberty. . . .
Constitution of North Carolina, Article XXI (1776).

❋   K-12 schools should implement an American Freedom Curriculum for all students in each grade

❋   Universities and colleges should require American history and civics, including the First Principles, especially for teacher preparation and professional development

❋   Law schools and bar exams should require and test American history and the First Principles

❋   Holidays should be reinvigorated with their original meaning and solemnity

❋   The media should cover and review current events using the First Principles and American history

❋   Existing and new nonprofit organizations should be dedicated to American history and civics, including the First Principles

❋   Politicians and voters should carefully consider history and the First Principles when voting and making policy

---

Political debate, from the Revolutionary period to the civil rights and gender equity eras, was framed by and rooted in arguments derived from our First Principles. Political debate today rarely if ever invokes them or even suggests much familiarity with them. Such vapid debate is unprincipled and superficial – and dangerous for our nation. Chief Justice of the Supreme Court and former Governor of California Earl Warren remarked that "liberty is not necessarily our permanent possession. Both external and internal pressures constantly assail it. It is axiomatic that every generation, to keep its freedom, must earn it through understanding the past, vigilance in the present and determination for the future."[306] As the Chief Justice predicted, our generation is facing its crisis and must earn its right to preserve our freedom. We can meet this challenge by vigorously implementing an agenda of strategic reform addressing many facets of our education system, society, and political culture. This part, therefore, outlines several complementary tactics by which we may reinvigorate our First Principles.

EDUCATION REFORM

The key to maintaining our liberty is an educated citizenry. Our system of self-government and the means by which our liberty is preserved should be of the utmost importance in education. Because our educational system is failing to meet the needs of too many students throughout the entire educational spectrum, comprehensive and wide-ranging reform is needed. Our students should start to learn our First Principles and American history in kindergarten; and such education should not end until they have graduated from high school or, if applicable, higher education. Education reform is the linchpin to preserving our freedoms.

The American Freedom Curriculum

The first obligation of our K-12 educational system should be to ground our young citizens in American civics and history, including the First Principles. Noah Webster, the famous publisher of the *Dictionary of the English Language* (1806), fittingly observed in an article advocating for the adoption of the Constitution, that "in no country, have the body of the people such knowledge of the rights of men and principles of government. This knowledge, joined with a keen sense of liberty and a watchful jealously, will guard our constitutions, and awaken the people to an instantaneous resistance of encroachments."[307]

Even at the dawn of the Constitution, however, the Founding Fathers were well aware that such principled comprehension would need to be fostered and expanded if the republic were to remain free. At his state's ratifying convention, Governor Samuel Huntington of Connecticut reflected the prevailing sentiment when he declared that "the people themselves must be the chief support of liberty. While the great body of freeholders are acquainted with the duties which they owe to their God, to themselves, and to men, they will remain free. But if ignorance and depravity should prevail, they will inevitably lead to slavery and ruin."

Concurring with Huntington, Thomas Jefferson, a visionary in the truest sense of the word regarding education, strongly advocated the establishment of public education by law and state constitutional amendment. Although he proposed such schools for many reasons, Jefferson explained in his influential *Notes on the State of Virginia* (1787), that the most important and legitimate reason was "that of rendering the people safe, as they are the ultimate guardians of their own liberty." He proposed that reading be learned through "chiefly historical" texts because understanding history was the key to protecting liberty:

> History by apprising them of the past will enable them to judge of the future; it will avail them of the experience of other times and other nations; it will qualify them to know ambition and designs of men; it will enable them to know ambition under every disguise it may assume; and knowing it, to defeat its views. In every government on earth is some trace of human weakness, some germ of corruption and degeneracy, which cunning will discover, and wickedness insensibly open, cultivate, and improve. Every government degenerates when trusted to the rulers of the people alone. The people themselves therefore are its only safe depositories. And to render even them safe their minds must be improved to a certain degree. This indeed is not all that is

necessary, though it be essentially necessary. An amendment of our constitution must here come in aid of the public education. The influence over government must be shared among the people. If every individual which composes their mass participates of the ultimate authority, the government will be safe. . . .

Until recently, as Chief Justice Warren opined, Americans nearly uniformly believed that our citizens could not "delegate to any or all of our governmental representatives the full responsibility for protection of our freedoms from the processes of erosion. Such protection can be had only through an understanding on the part of individual citizens of what these freedoms are, how they came into being and whether their spirit dominates our institutions and the life of our country."[308] To fulfill our "enormous legacy," Senator Barack Obama more recently reflected, requires us to "recognize our history. . . . [U]nderstanding our history and knowing what it means is an everyday activity."[309]

Instead of running from or castigating America, our educators should provide all of our students an excellent grounding in our form of self-government, including its historical and philosophical underpinnings – with a special emphasis on our First Principles. Our students should also develop the ability to fully and thoughtfully participate in the political process. Although there are some noble and excellent efforts to address these challenges, the reality is that current educational efforts are too weak, disparate, dispersed, and diluted to make the dramatic changes we need.

To address this educational crisis, each state should establish and implement an American Freedom Curriculum. This Curriculum should have specific, measurable expectations for students in each grade from kindergarten through the end of high school. The American Freedom Curriculum should teach all students: (i) the rule of law; (ii) the recognition and protection of the unalienable rights of individuals; (iii) equality; (iv) the Social Compact; and (v) the protection of unalienable rights as the legitimate purpose and limit of government. Focusing on the First Principles, the curriculum should comprehensively address civics, American history, and comparative political science.

Preferably the American Freedom Curriculum would be taught in a multidisciplinary way that truly engages students. It would emphasize the search for truth, critical thinking, collaborative learning, and self-directed, student-centered learning.[310] Properly leveraging Information Age tools and learning practices would dramatically enhance this effort.[311] The control exercised by textbook publishers should also be leveraged by establishing state standards that implement the American Freedom Curriculum.

Annual assessment and testing should also be a component of the American Freedom Curriculum. The federal No Child Left Behind Act currently requires testing in 3rd-8th grade in math and reading, and will eventually include science. However, the federal government has deemed that civics and history are not so important as to merit such testing. This myopic policy has had the unintended consequence of reducing history and civics instruction since the federally tested subjects are given higher priority in the classroom.[312] Of course students need to read, write, and compute. Unfortunately, by making social studies the step-child of federal policy, our students might be able to read the *Declaration of Independence*, but they may very well have no idea what it means, how it has influenced our history, or why it matters today. Despite the federal government's conclusion to the contrary, annual assessment in American history and civics should be a high priority. A focused, short test with on-line results would likely best serve educators and students. By coupling the American Freedom Curriculum with annual testing for each grade, we can best ensure that American history, civics, and the First Principles receive the attention our students deserve.

Third or fourth graders should be able to identify, if not recite the introductory portions of the *Declaration of Independence*. George Washington, John Adams, James Madison, Thomas Jefferson, Thomas Paine, Susan B. Anthony, Elizabeth Cady Stanton, Abraham Lincoln, and Dr Martin Luther King, Jr should become familiar figures in grade school. No later than the end of elementary school, students should be able to describe the basic features of the American government and the First Principles. The republican nature of our government, the separation of powers, federalism, the Bill of Rights, judicial review, and the sovereignty of the people should be well-understood concepts in middle school. No later than the end of middle school, our students should comprehend the contours of American history, including the causes and effects of the Revolution, the War of 1812, Manifest Destiny and the fate of Native Americans, the Civil War, the Spanish American War, the Progressive Movement, World Wars I and II, the New Deal, the Civil Rights Movement and Great Society, the Korean and Vietnam Wars, the Cold War, the Reagan Revolution, the Gulf War, and the War on Terror. In high school our students should be learning deep concepts; debating policies of all parties in light of principles; role playing; writing position papers; speaking in public; asking hard questions; conducting research; participating in public service; and even creating disciplinary knowledge.

With a robust American Freedom Curriculum, when it is time to vote and engage in the political arena, our graduates would understand the wonderful blessing they have by being citizens of the United States of America. When they are called upon to defend the country, they would have a heartfelt and reasoned understanding that such service is for something much different than conquest or vainglory, but for freedom. And if called to duty for something other than the defense of freedom, those called would be well-equipped to challenge the cause. Such an educational program would best fan the flame of freedom for generations to come.

Restoring the First Principles and History in Higher Education

Although K-12 reform is indispensable, so is reform in higher education. Most political, cultural, social, business, and media leaders attend the academy, and all but abandoning our First Principles and history in higher education is a recipe for ignorant leadership.

When attending the Continental Congress, John Adams wrote to his confidant James Warren that "Our great complaint is the scarcity of men fit to govern such mighty interests as are clashing in the present contest. . . . Our policy must be to improve every opportunity and means for forming our people, and preparing leaders for them in the grand march of politics."[313] To meet this challenge, not only should the states adopt the American Freedom Curriculum, all institutions of higher education should require at least one full-year course in American history. These courses should provide intensive focus on the American Revolution and the establishing of the Constitution.

In addition, all college and university students should be required to attend at least one semester of American political science or civics. Like K-12 reform, these courses should focus not on seat-time, but on quality. They should probe deeply into the American experience and principles, and students should become well-versed in the primary documents of the American

Revolution, the forming of the Constitution, and the civil rights movements. These courses should ensure that our most educated citizens are effectively prepared to meaningfully participate in our system of government. Moreover, students should be able to apply that foundational knowledge to today's controversies.

Institutions that currently struggle with these topics should follow the practices of those schools that provide exemplary education in such arenas. Colorado State University, Rhodes College, Calvin College, Grove City College, University of Colorado (Boulder), University of New Mexico, Spring Arbor University, George Mason University, Hillsdale College, and other universities and colleges recognized for excellence in history and civics should be studied and emulated (and, of course, improved upon). Although some of these exemplars may not be generally considered to be elite institutions, they have stellar results compared to many of their more prestigious brethren.[314]

Moreover, colleges and universities should create academic centers – including community outreach programs – dedicated to promoting deeper knowledge and research regarding American civics and history. As the Intercollegiate Studies Institute's American Civic Literacy Program has revealed, such efforts have been widespread in other areas; and establishing new centers focused on the First Principles, American history, and civics "would act as resource catalysts on campus for improving the teaching of American history, political science, and economics."[315] One such extant program is Hillsdale College's Hoogland Center, which hosts seminars for K-12 teachers to help them become better teachers by gaining a deeper understanding of American history. Similarly, Wayne State University's Center for the Study of Citizenship hosts conferences and promotes research and intellectual exchange regarding the meaning of citizenship. Today, these centers are rare exceptions. Universities and colleges need to establish and expand such efforts so that they become an integral part of any institution of higher education.

Teacher Preparation
and Development Reform

Simply put, too many of our colleges and universities do a poor job of preparing our teacher corps in American history and civics. Although there are many fine social studies teachers, many struggle with basic concepts and are ill-equipped to meaningfully engage their students.[316] The American Freedom Curriculum and higher education reform will only succeed if our teachers and professors are well-prepared to provide instructional leadership to students. Thus, our state boards and departments of education, as well as colleges and universities, need to revamp teacher preparation programs to improve the quality, rigor, and understanding of the First Principles, American history, and civics.

Moreover, with millions of teachers already in the workforce, teachers must be given strong and various opportunities to engage in professional development centered on these critical areas. Nonprofits and educational institutions should follow the Hoogland Center's lead and help our current teachers build upon their current knowledge and skills. Improved teacher preparation and development will be indispensable to improving the quality of instruction and student learning.

LEGAL REFORM:
LAW SCHOOL AND BAR REFORM

Chief Justice Warren long ago reminded us that "A dedicated bench and a militant bar are the natural leaders" to preserving our liberties. "Without an independent judiciary there can be no freedom. . . . Without a militant bar to assert in court the constitutional rights of individuals regardless of how unpopular those assertions might be at the moment, such rights become merely 'sounding brass and tinkling cymbals.'"[317] Lawyers have a special trust and duty to maintain our freedoms, and care must be taken to ensure that they are capable of fulfilling that task. The profound English parliamentarian Edmund Burke observed that Americans possessed a "fierce spirit of liberty" that was "stronger . . . probably than in any other people of the earth" in part because of Americans' widespread knowledge of the law. Burke explained that "This study renders men acute, inquisitive, dextrous, prompt in attack, ready in defence, full of resources. In other countries, the people, more simple, and of a less mercurial cast, judge of an ill principle in government only by an actual grievance; here they anticipate the evil, and judge of the pressure of the grievance by the badness of the principle. They augur misgovernment at a distance, and snuff the approach of tyranny in every tainted breeze."[318]

What was once prized and thought to enliven our spirit is now ignored or derided in the very institutions that should most celebrate them. Most law professors pay no attention to American history in their courses, and many scorn the Founding Fathers. Likewise, the First Principles are generally ignored or, when noticed, distorted or denigrated. Legal education, especially at elite institutions, focuses on fashionable legal doctrines and trendy critiques or distortions of the Constitution. There is nothing wrong with exploring these doctrines and the shortfalls in American law; but to do so in the absence of a significant and fair focus on the First Principles and history is misleading and undermines our system of ordered liberty.

Like K-12 and higher education in general, law schools must refocus their curriculum to include the First Principles and their generating history. Some might consider this beneath such institutions. To the contrary, constitutional law is often considered the most enlightened and elevated of legal topics. The real problem is that such education today is often devoid of any meaningful connection to the Founding Fathers, the Constitution, or American history. As a very significant source of learning for our political class, law schools have a special obligation to ensure that their students receive a comprehensive education regarding our constitutional order. Law schools, therefore, should mandate at least one year of constitutional law (many do). More importantly, law schools should require the extensive study of the First Principles as well as the history surrounding the American Revolution, the adoption of the Constitution, and the civil rights movements. The American Bar Association should include such a requirement in its law school accreditation criteria.

In addition, state bar exams and the Multi-State Bar Exam should include testing on the First Principles. No lawyer should be licensed to practice law without understanding that our nation was founded on the rule of law, the recognition and protection of the unalienable rights of individuals, equality, the Social Compact, and the protection of unalienable rights as the legitimate purpose and limit of government.

REVIVING OUR HOLIDAYS

On July 10, 1858, Lincoln spoke of the importance of celebrating Independence Day:

> We are now a mighty nation. . . . We run our memory back over the pages of history for about eighty-two years and we discover that we were then a very small people in point of numbers . . . with vastly less of everything we deem desirable among men, we look upon the change as exceedingly advantageous to us and our posterity, and we fix upon something that happened away back. . . . We find a race of men living in that day whom we claim as our fathers and grandfathers; they were iron men, they fought for the principle that they were contending for; and we understood that by what they then did it has followed that the degree of posterity that we now enjoy has come to us. We hold this annual celebration to remind ourselves of all the good done in this process of time of how it was done and who did it, and how we are historically connected with it; and we go from these meetings in better humor with ourselves – we feel more attached the one to the other, and more firmly bound to the country we inhabit. In every way we are better men in the age, and race, and country in which we live for these celebrations.[319]

Today's stark reality is that our holidays have generally become an empty excuse for a day off, thread worn retail sales, and enjoyable social gatherings. These activities usually lack any acknowledgement of the underlying and solemn importance of the days.

Independence Day (July 4th) is perhaps the most vivid example. Fireworks, hotdogs, and apple pie fill the day. The Spirit of '76, however, has nearly disappeared. On July 3, 1776, just one day after independence was approved (but one day prior to the formal adoption of the *Declaration of Independence*), John Adams presciently understood that the anniversary of Independence Day would be marked by "pomp and parade, shows, games, sports, guns, bells, bonfires, and illuminations, from one end of this continent to the other, from this time forward, forever more." What is missing today was Adams' conjoined expectation that "It ought to be commemorated as the day of deliverance, by solemn acts of devotion to God Almighty. It ought to be solemnized. . . ."[320] We have the hamburgers and parades, but any solemnization is trite.

Likewise, Presidents' Day is an empty exercise for commercials with salesman dressed like Washington and Lincoln to hawk their wares at "unprecedented" discounts. Veterans Day and Memorial Day follow the general pattern, minus the costumed salesmen. Some holidays have a traditional parade, but again they are usually divorced from the underlying holiday. Although some academic gatherings mark Martin Luther King, Jr Day, that is the exception. The situation is so desperate that the federal government recently decreed a "Constitution Day" (September 17, the anniversary of the signing of the Constitution) to require any school accepting federal funds to teach about the Constitution on that day.

Schools, media, businesses, theatre groups, civic groups, and others should leverage the opportunities of each holiday and make them teachable moments. Independence Day should be chock full of readers of the *Declaration of Independence* in malls, town halls, and parades. Veterans should march proudly in parades on their special day. Lincoln-Douglas debate reenactments should pepper Presidents' Day, as should readings of Washington's *Farwell Address*. The *I Have a Dream* speech should ring proudly over the radio and television on Martin Luther King, Jr Day. Constitution Day should be celebrated in all schools. Television, radio, magazines, websites, and newspapers should provide extensive coverage of the origins, purposes, and importance of the holidays.

Although these commemorations may present little that is new, as Chief Justice Warren explained, they would "still serve a purpose of rekindling the spirit evinced by" the Founding Fathers "and in recharging our minds with the high purposes that impelled them to contribute so much to the society in which we live and to the institutions which guard our well-being. They afford us the opportunity to say in unison, 'Lest we forget.'"[321] These activities would be meaningful, engaging, and thoughtful reminders of the exceptional nature of America and the blessings of freedom we still enjoy. By routinely reinvigorating our understanding and the spirit of our First Principles and history, they would create a ready wellspring to preserve our republic in times of trouble and crisis.

MEDIA REORIENTATION

Jefferson wrote that "The basis of our governments being the opinion of the people, the very first object should be to keep that right; and were it left to me to decide whether we should have a government without newspapers or newspapers without a government, I should not hesitate a moment to prefer the latter."[322] Indeed, not long ago many called the free press the "fourth estate" – akin to a separate branch of government that ensured fairness, integrity, and good public policy. In light of the importance and confidence placed in the press by the Founding Fathers, they would likely be sorely disappointed today. With some notable exceptions, for far too long the media have blithely reported on politics and current events with superficiality and a sound-bite mentality.

Perhaps some in the media are beginning to awaken to the abysmal state of journalism. Some talk show hosts, like Mitch Albom, Paul W. Smith, and Frank Beckmann of WJR 760 AM in Detroit, have become very critical of the general media's obsession with celebrity, the frivolous, and the trite. Moreover, one core news outlet appears disconcerted with at least some of its coverage. On the last weekend of February, 2007 the Associated Press engaged in an experimental blackout of one of America's notorious celebrities to gauge its effect. Predictably, the celebrity engaged in what appeared to be petty criminal conduct; yet, the failure to report her misbehavior was not missed. Nevertheless, the Associated Press story reporting the blackout admitted that it had provoked internal controversy about self-censorship, and the blackout was lifted. In other words, a weekend without reporting on the misdeeds of one vacuous celebrity in one news outlet was apparently just too much for the republic to bear.[323] In fact, she dominated the news just a few months later with new, all but inevitable escapades.

Moreover, although many columnists, blogs, and talk show hosts engage in meaningful commentary and critical review, they only very rarely examine the issues of the day through the prism of our history or First Principles. Journalists and commentators would much better serve the public and themselves if they began to do so. In a parallel fashion, the consumers of the media should demand that the media begin to use such a perspective. Voting with our pocketbook will gain the attention of the media and spark change. Public outrage over outlandish comments has resulted in the dismissal of major media figures. The same forces can compel meaningful reform in the media.

Asking probing questions and reporting how policy proposals or actions square with equality, the rule of law, the Social Compact, unalienable rights, and limited government would be a significant and vital contribution to the political dialogue and health of the republic. For example, if the Surgeon General were to advocate that the federal government impose a tax on fast food high in fat content, one could be certain that the firestorm in today's media would not focus on American history or our First Principles. To the contrary, we could expect harsh and bitter commentary on all sides of the debate (health professionals likely advocating for one position, with the restaurant industry on the other, just to name two).

Clearly the discussion would be liberally peppered with sarcasm and comic relief. However, focusing first on whether such a policy would advance or denigrate our First Principles and history would elevate and illuminate the political dialogue. Would such a policy conflict with the rule of law? How does the policy advance or conflict with the unalienable rights of citizens? Is the purpose of government advanced or undermined by the policy? Would a proposal to further expand the authority of the federal Food and Drug Administration conflict with federalism and enumerated powers? Can the policy be reconciled with limited government? What impact could the policy have on equality? Is the policy expanding the authority of the federal government in ways that would have been opposed by the Founders, or is it simply the natural progression of the federal government's long-standing role in commerce, health, and safety?

People could honestly and vigorously disagree on the answers to these questions. For example, one could argue that by advancing the health of the unsuspecting public, the policy protects unalienable rights (i.e., the right to life); another could argue that the policy overreaches the limited authority of government and undermines the unalienable right to pursue happiness by empowering a nanny state. Although people would likely disagree, by forcing policy makers and the public to think about these issues in light of our history and First Principles, the terms of the debate would be radically changed – for the better.

Another pertinent example is the recent controversy over the detainment of "enemy combatants" by the United States military for very lengthy periods of time without trial. Today's news coverage and political debate often devolved to the point where opponents of the detainment policy stopped just short of calling the government fascist, while supporters of the policy stopped just short of calling the opponents aiders and abetters of terrorists. A review of the issue in light of our First Principles would have better grounded the heated argument into a meaningful discussion. For example, opponents of the policy should have confronted a threshold issue - why should foreign nationals have any rights when they are not part of the Social Compact? After all, how can those who can be carpet bombed on the battlefield be entitled to a lawyer? On the other hand, supporters of the policy should have been forced to address why the Geneva Conventions (*i.e.*, the rule of law) should not apply to the detainees and how the detentions are not in direct conflict with due process and other fundamental protections.

Another example of where more informed media scrutiny would be helpful is the current controversy regarding the medicinal use of marijuana and its legalization (or decriminalization) in several of the states. Conservatives who generally favor limited government tend to support a very active federal role in stopping efforts to permit the legalization of drugs, while liberals who are often very supportive of federal intervention in many aspects of our daily lives argue that this is a matter for the states. Conservatives generally support the federal government's criminalization of marijuana that is grown and consumed in accord with the law of a state, which never crosses state lines, which is prescribed by a doctor, and is only used for personal use. How do conservatives support their view in light of federalism and enumerated powers? On the other hand, how can liberals who have historically supported very similar laws in connection with agriculture (they support prohibitions on growing wheat by farmers to feed their own families to bolster price supports) defend attacking the same mechanisms when used to ban a historically illegal drug?

Similarly, supporters and opponents of new federal programs would be forced to discuss the rationale for such policies. How would a new program involving education or regulation of technology, for example, comport with federalism and enumerated power? Would such programs appropriately fall within the federal government's purview over interstate commerce, or would it infringe on the rights of the people and the states? Providing more in-depth coverage regarding tax policy, presidential and congressional elections, judicial appointments, appropriation bills, social controversies, and armed conflicts in the context of the First Principles would enlighten policy makers and the public when grappling with such issues. Such coverage would enable voters and policy makers to seriously consider the appropriateness of proposed policies instead of relying on sound-bite propaganda to influence their positions on the issues.

Moreover, a review of our history in connection with media coverage would enlighten the discussion and better equip the public and others to address current controversies. We need only turn to the presidential election of 2000 for a very vivid example. Contrary to early polling returns, Republican Governor George W. Bush appeared to have captured the electoral votes of Florida by the slimmest of margins, thereby winning the presidency. However, Vice President Gore and the Democrats cried foul and argued that certain votes were not appropriately cast because of their confusing format (the so called butterfly ballot being the main purported culprit). Other ballots, the Democrats argued, were erroneously counted (or not) because they were physically defective (or not).

While the nation was enraptured by hanging chads and vote recounts, the media all but ignored an extraordinary parallel situation in the election of 1876. As noted in Part II, that election took place between Governor Rutherford B. Hayes of Ohio and Governor Samuel J. Tilden of New York. The electoral votes of several states – including Florida – were vigorously disputed. Like the Bush-Gore election's notorious butterfly ballots, the Hayes-Tilden election involved controversial ballots – many Democrat ballots had Republican President Abraham Lincoln's face printed on them. In the Hayes-Tilden election, Congress created a fifteen member electoral commission to make recommendations to Congress about the electoral votes of four states. In a series of 8-7 votes the commission awarded all disputed electoral votes to Hayes. Congress accepted the commission's decision and Hayes became President. Clearly this rich and controversial history could have been drawn upon (or rejected) by policy makers and the public in connection with the crisis facing the nation in the 2000 election, but it was all but universally ignored.

Nearly all policy issues can be subjected to media examination in light of our history and First Principles. This can only lead to an improved understanding of the real issues we face and how to best address them within the framework of our free nation. Meaningful and insightful reform by the media is a critical step to protecting America's freedoms.

EXPANDING INFORMATIVE NONPROFIT ACTIVITY

That Washington, D.C., and to a lesser extent the state capitals, are awash with lobbyists and special interests is so obvious that hardly anyone bothers to notice. Almost every conceivable special interest group is well-organized and attempts to influence policy making and legislation through intensive lobbying and campaigning. Other than a few notable think tanks and similar organizations, the lobbyists run roughshod over constitutional principles and the greater good while seeking to obtain their goals and objectives.

One method to counteract these countless pressure points is by supporting and expanding nonprofit organizations that strive to advance learning of, and policy making informed by, American history and First Principles. Such nonprofits could aid in educational efforts for students, voters, media, policy makers, and others. Furthermore, such nonprofits could actively seek to ensure that principles and history are considered and evaluated when the issues of the day are addressed. In other words, these nonprofits could reinject the importance of our history and First Principles in policy making when no other voices would do so. The few nonprofits which currently strive to do so should be vigorously supported and expanded; and new nonprofits with varying concentrations of interests should be created and encouraged.

With no intention of excluding others (and with apologies of the first order), noteworthy nonprofit organizations which could be supported or emulated include the Michigan Center for Civic Education,[324] the Student Statesman Institute, The National Conference on Citizenship, the Center for Information and Research on Civic Learning and Engagement (CIRCLE), the Alexander Hamilton Project at The New York Historical Society, the Michigan Council for the Social Studies, the American Civic Literacy Program of the Intercollegiate Studies Institute (ISI), and ISI's Jack Miller Center for the Teaching of America's Founding Principles.

Individual nonprofits could focus on the rule of law, unalienable rights, the Social Compact, limited government, or equality. Others could focus on various historical eras, critical personalities, different branches of government, or the Bill of Rights. Moreover, although there are some excellent history museums, they tend to focus on facts and figures, not the underlying spirit of America. Creating (or reorienting) museums and historical attractions to focus on the First Principles and the philosophy underpinning our historical development would also contribute mightily to the effort. The Henry Ford Museum's *With Liberty and Justice for All* is one such exhibit. A robust and vigorous nonprofit sector could effectively move the terms of the political dialogue to include the historical and principled perspective in policy making and governance.

ENGAGING THE POLITICAL DISCOURSE AND INFLUENCING POLICY MAKING

We must make the First Principles relevant in our political discourse. For far too long our politicians, activists, media, academics, think tanks, educators, voters, and general public have ignored if not denigrated them. Social programs are enacted and dismantled; taxes raised and slashed; bureaucracies created and reinvented; armies deployed and recalled; civil rights and national security measures enacted and repealed; constitutional amendments proposed and defeated; and critical court decisions rendered and reversed – all without as much as a whisper of the First Principles and the manner in which they are woven into our constitutional structure.

Immediately following the adoption of the *Declaration of Independence*, the people of Pennsylvania adopted a constitution that explained "That a frequent recurrence to fundamental principles, and a firm adherence to justice, moderation, temperance, industry, and frugality, are absolutely necessary to preserve the blessings of liberty, and keep a government free: The people ought therefore to pay particular attention to these points in the choice of officers and representatives, and have a right to exact a due and constant regard to them, from their legislatures and magistrates, in the making and executing such laws as are necessary for the good government of the State."[325] Several other revolutionary-era state constitutions echo this pronouncement.[326] Rush was more blunt – he supported the creation of public schools because each citizen "must watch the state as if its liberties depended on his vigilance alone. . . ."[327] We desperately need to heed this wise counsel. Contrary to the prevailing view, the First Principles remain exceptionally enlightening to the discussions of the day – only if someone were to use the illumination they provide.

New and current proposals regarding government programs and policies could be examined in light of the rule of law, equality, and the protection of unalienable rights. As explained in Part II, the First Principles are specifically the basis of our form of government, and current issues should also be evaluated in light of that form of government. For example, a new proposed federal law to criminalize murder that involves no interstate conduct (there is no such law today) could be evaluated in light of federalism, separation of powers, checks and balances, enumerated powers, and the purpose of government. Would the new federal murder law ignore or embrace the constitutional precept of federalism? Is the law within the enumerated powers of the federal government? Does the federalization of murder provide too much authority to the executive branch or fail to ensure proper oversight? Is the federal murder law a complete break with historical limits on federal authority or a fulfillment of the fundamental purpose of government – the protection of the unalienable right of life?

Proposals to address healthcare reform should be reviewed with similar scrutiny. Such proposals today range from nationalizing healthcare from one extreme (*i.e.*, the government would take control of the entire industry) to completely eliminating government intervention on the other extreme (*i.e.*, eliminating federal programs such as Medicaid, Medicare, and Social Security). Would such proposals advance or undermine the purpose of government? Which proposal best preserves federalism? Would nationalizing healthcare exceed the federal government's enumerated powers and infringe federalism; or could state programs be enacted to meet any such concerns? Would vesting decision making over individuals' medical care to a government bureaucracy undermine or further the principle of republican government? Would equality be hindered, supported, or unaffected? Is the philosophy of the Social Compact strengthened or weakened by nationalization or eliminating government intervention? Can equality be furthered, or denigrated, by any of the proposals?

The current controversy over federal "earmarks" (i.e., specific pork barrel projects") could also be evaluated using the First Principles and our history. The media report that these earmarks are slipped into congressional appropriations in the dead of the night and approved with hardly a member of Congress understanding that the appropriation was being enacted; and earmarks became rampant in Congress by 2006. On the other hand, members of Congress defend this process because earmarks do not increase actual spending but only allow a member of Congress to designate already allocated funds for a specific project at the behest of his or her constituents. Is this the thoughtful deliberative process the Founders believed would be implemented by the Congress – especially the Senate? Would Washington, Adams, and Jefferson been pleased to know that such practices are not only condoned but standard operating procedure? How does this earmark process affect the legitimacy of the rule of law, the republican form of government, and the Social Compact? Has bi-cameralism failed in this context? What of checks and balances? Is Madison's theory of faction countering faction undermined by this practice? As noted in Part II, President Madison vetoed the Bonus Bill that would have set aside $1,500,000 as a permanent fund for internal improvements because it was outside of the scope of the federal government's enumerated powers. Today a single earmark in an unread omnibus bill of thousands of pages spends more than the Bonus Bill without a second thought. Have we gone astray?

Military policy and foreign affairs could likewise be examined using this framework. One could question how America's overseas commitments in any given part of the world relate to limited government, the rule of law, and the protection of unalienable rights. Whether the military's recruitment and retention policies favor or undermine equality and due process could also be asked. Tax policies could undergo scrutiny under due process, limited government, rule of law, and equality principles. Homeland security proposals could be reviewed in light of unalienable rights, judicial review, and Social Compact concerns. Judicial appointments could be evaluated in light of the proper role of judicial review and potential appointees' understanding of the constitutional order.

Such an approach sets the general terms of the debate within proper parameters of decision making. Because current political discussion ignores such issues, today's free-wheeling, sound-bite ridden discussion masks fundamental issues and questions. The current debate inevitably denigrates our

First Principles and erodes American traditions. Only by asking the right questions and appropriately framing the issues can we hope to improve our political dialogue and public policy.

Indeed, the very first questions that should be raised about legislation, court rulings, administrative actions, and similar matters are whether they foster or violate the First Principles. Similarly, whether such actions are in fidelity with or contrary to the system established to maintain the First Principles – *i.e.*, the sovereignty of the people, republicanism, separation of powers, checks and balances, judicial review, the Bill of Rights, checking of factions, enumerated powers, and federalism – should be seriously explored.

Not only should our political dialogue include our First Principles, reviewing current affairs in light of our history offers significant perspective and insight. When faced with military attacks in the past, for example, Americans have been willing to make enormous sacrifices to preserve our freedom. In the Civil War, Union soldiers suffered over 600,000 casualties. American casualties in World War I totaled over 300,000; World War II over 1,000,000; Korea over 100,000; and Vietnam over 150,000. As of May, 2007 American casualties in the Iraq War were approximately 25,000 (with a much lower proportion of deaths as compared to prior conflicts). Most of these wars were highly successful, but the guerilla war of Vietnam was a colossal failure. Iraq is an open question. On the other hand, some highly successful military interventions and wars involved a very low loss of life, time, and expenditures, but with large returns. Such confrontations include the intervention with the Barbary States under Jefferson; the invasion of Panama and extradition of General Manuel Noriega under President George Herbert Walker Bush; the Spanish American War under President William McKinley; and the invasion of Grenada under Reagan. Perhaps our greatest success – the Cold War and the internal collapse of the USSR – was won with no direct military engagement. Following World War II, under America's leadership, fascist and imperial regimes were altered into strong free republics. However, the populations of Japan, Italy, and Germany had been severely attacked for years and they unconditionally surrendered to a united front of the Allies which dominated the political and military sphere of the conquered and subsequently transformed the countries for decades. Indeed, more than fifty years later, American troops continue to be stationed in Japan, Italy, Korea, and Germany. In addition, the history of the Middle East is full of warfare, internecine conflict, and national boundaries all but arbitrarily created by imperial powers.

As the Iraq War began – and now drags on – one could rightfully wonder if any of this history was meaningfully and appropriately considered by the proponents, opponents, strategists, and tacticians of the effort. The media utterly ignore such context. These historical precedents, of course, do not necessarily resolve any political debate, but they do provide a valuable sense of context and proportionality to the debates. More important, they serve as invaluable reference points to develop American successes and to avoid fatal pitfalls.

Of course, there will often be disagreements regarding the application of the First Principles, history, and the Constitution to specific policy questions. However, as Jefferson masterfully explained in the aftermath of an extremely bitter partisan election in 1800, "every difference of opinion is not a difference of principle. We have been called by different names brethren of the same principle. We are all Republicans, we are all Federalists."[328] We should not expect that simply by examining issues in light of the First Principles and our history that all will come to the same conclusions. Like an effort to tax high-fat fast food, there would likely be significant disagreement about the application of our First Principles to any particular issues – but the exercise is critical to ensuring that the dialogue is informed and maintains the American system of government. Moreover, some issues will likely be resolved definitively because the First Principles will provide clear answers. In any event, by failing to demand of ourselves this critical review of public policy, our nation deprives itself of the most penetrating analysis possible, and all but ensures that our republic will fatally drift away from its First Principles.

We must critically ask whether our politicians, judges, bureaucrats, activists, editorial writers, journalists, academics, and think tanks understand the First Principles and historical basis of our freedoms, and whether their actions and participation in the American constitutional order are grounded in such understandings. In addition to asking whether they are following our First Principles, we must demand that they do so and hold them accountable when they do not. If these crucial actors do not base their decisions, opinions, analysis, and actions upon the First Principles and the system established to maintain them, then there is little reason to hope that America will long remain free.

The people in America are sovereign. Our political leaders serve at our pleasure. In the end even the bureaucracies are controlled by elections. The appointment and election of judges is also under the direct or indirect control of the body politic. The media are hyper-responsive to the purchasing decisions and tastes of consumers. The reputations and funding of think tanks and academics is directly related to their credibility in the eyes of the public and the political class. Our standards should be high; our expectations deliberate; our choices thoughtful. We need not settle for those who care not about our history or First Principles; we certainly should not embrace those who ignore, denigrate, or disdain them. If we do, our fate is sealed.

Conclusion
The Choice

[W]e know that we are not helpless prisoners of history. We are free men. President Dwight Eisenhower, *First Inaugural Address* (1953).

Our nation established a government of First Principles so that we might live as free men and women. Of course, we have never totally fulfilled our aspiration. The Founding Fathers, for instance, enforced slavery, discriminated against women, and denied the vote to un-propertied white men. Each successive generation has also fallen short. After all, the true implications of fully realizing our First Principles have often remained hidden or unacknowledged for decades or even generations. Yet, when those implications are understood and embraced, they inspire nearly miraculous changes in our society – and in Western Civilization. Whether America will continue its long march of freedom or retreat is the critical question facing our generation.

All that our nation has accomplished is now at grave risk. If this book reveals nothing else, it is the uniqueness of the American experience. For most of human history, freedom has been the exception. To be free is a rare and precious gift. Our liberty is the result of centuries of struggle, bought with the blood of our forefathers. During the Cold War, we placed the entire nation and world on the brink of nuclear annihilation rather than submit to communist tyranny.

On the eve of the American Revolution, Dr Joseph Warren vividly expressed the prevailing sentiment of the Founding Fathers when he wrote in *The Suffolk Resolves* that there "is an indispensable duty which we owe to God, our country and posterity, by all lawful ways and means in our power to maintain, defend and preserve those civil and religious rights and liberties, for which many of our fathers fought, bled and died, and to hand them down entire to future generations." We are the heirs of that duty. The time has come for this generation to fully heed this call. We must act now to reinvigorate our destiny as a free people.

We must continue the struggle not only for ourselves, but for the future generations of the world. The world's only superpower, America will in large measure determine the destiny of all peoples. George Washington's warning to the nation in his *First Inaugural Address* (1789) rings as true today as it did then: "the preservation of the sacred fire of liberty and the destiny of the republican model of government are justly considered, perhaps, as *deeply*, as *finally*, staked on the experiment entrusted to the hands of the American people."

This work provides the mechanism by which we can choose to remain free. The crisis is clearly diagnosed in Part I. We have the indisputable documentation by which to alert our fellow citizens of the crisis. Any reasonable doubts about the depth and extent of our ignorance and disdain should be erased. Share the data in Part I with your friends, families, media, business leaders, educators, politicians, agencies, opinion leaders, nonprofit organizations, religious leaders, and others. The first step to preventing our republic's suicide is making the people fully aware of the crisis.

Part III provides specific recommendations that we can undertake to meet the challenge. We can lobby our local and state education leaders and legislators to ensure that an American Freedom Curriculum is adopted. We can demand that teacher preparation institutions and state boards of education require teachers to be well-versed in American history, civics, and the First Principles. We can support political candidates who recognize the primary importance of the First Principles, and oppose those who do not. If you are a lawyer – or even if you are not – you can propose adding the First Principles to the American Bar Association's accreditation standards, the Multi-State Bar Exam, and your state's bar exam. We can demand more informed and comprehensive coverage from local newspapers and the media in general. We can donate to appropriate nonprofits or volunteer to help (or even start) one. We can demand that schools create meaningful holiday programs, and we can start or support new holiday traditions. We can write opinion pieces, pen letters to policy makers and educators, and engage in on-line blog discussions. We can purchase this book for others and ask them to become involved.

Part II provides the essential philosophical and historical information needed to make a difference. We can use the information in Part II to meaningfully engage in the political process. The political class should use Part II to refocus their campaigns, policy making, and decisions. Media should use Part II to reorient and reenergize their coverage. If you are an educator, you can use Part II to change your lesson plans, curricula, standards, and assessments. You can assign this book as required reading. Parents can demand that the educators incorporate the content of Part II in their instruction. Taxpayers can use Part II to evaluate the effectiveness of their K-12 schools, higher education, politicians, museums, and media. Leverage Part II to improve holiday traditions. Higher education institutions should outline course content and requirements in light of Part II. Nonprofits can draw upon Part II to refocus or begin new initiatives and programs involving American history and the First Principles.

The tools for our survival are in this book. Everyone can do something, no matter how small. The avenues for engagement are nearly limitless. Pick one, or several, but do not simply toss this book to the side and do nothing – you might as well be putting the hemlock to your lips. Even modest activities by many can coalesce to trigger fundamental reform. In our apathetic environment, the committed and vigorous can rise to the top and dramatically change the societal and political dynamic. The question we face as free citizens of the American republic is whether we will take the time and energy to preserve our liberty.

Are we, the heirs of the Revolution, willing to allow our freedom to fade out meekly, or will we boldly reclaim our heritage and maintain our liberty? Have we won the wars against monarchy, imperialism, fascism, and communism so that we may timidly lose our freedom to complacency, ignorance, and disdain of our founding principles? If we are unconcerned about freedom, if we are frightened of responsibility, if we are content to surrender our liberties, if we cower at the thought of defending our rights, if we delight in forfeiting our liberty and relish becoming unfree, then we should succumb to ignorance, complacency, and disdain. If we savor our freedom, if we rejoice in our responsibility, if we will fight for our liberty, if we reject the idea of tamely losing our rights, if we would rather die free than live as slaves, then we must take up the banner of the First Principles and ensure that they are known and prevail throughout the land today and in future generations. The choice is ours.

Endnotes

[1] See, *e.g.*, Steve Farkas, Jean Johnson, and Ann Duffett, *Knowing It By Heart, Americans Consider the Constitution and its Meaning*, A Report by Public Agenda for the National Constitution Center (Philadelphia, Pennsylvania: 2002). See also several other citations throughout this Chapter.

[2] Tom W. Smith and Seokho Kim, *National Pride in Cross-National and Temporal Perspective*, National Opinion Research Center/University of Chicago, International Journal of Public Opinion Research, 18 (Spring, 2006), pp. 127-136.

[3] The National Anthem Project (2006).

[4] The Gallup Organization, National Telephone Survey of 1,014 Adults Conducted June 28-July 1, 2001, cited in *Knowing It By Heart, Americans Consider the Constitution and its Meaning*, p. 14.

[5] Sheapardson Stern & Kaminsky (sponsored by the National Constitution Center), Constitutional Knowledge Survey (poll conducted September 1997), cited in *Knowing It By Heart, Americans Consider the Constitution and its Meaning*, p. 14.

[6] *Americans' Awareness of First Amendment Freedoms*, McCormick Tribune Freedom Museum (Chicago, Illinois: 2006).

[7] *Ibid.*

[8] Harris Interactive Market Research, *Civics Education*, prepared for The American Bar Association (Chicago, Illinois: 2005).

[9] See, *e.g.*, *Ibid.*

[10] *Democracy at Risk: Renewing the Political Science of Citizenship*, Report of the American Political Science Association's Standing Committee on Civic Education and Engagement, Final Draft for Review, Annual Meeting of the American Political Science Association, September 2-5 (Chicago, Illinois: 2004), p. 1. See also Carnegie Corporation of New York and The Center for Information and Research on Civic Learning and Engagement (CIRCLE), *The Civic Mission of Schools* (New York, New York: 2003), pp. 18-20.

[11] Emmanuel Oritsejafor and James Guseh, *Civic Education Among College Students: A Case Study* (North Carolina Central University: Undated), p. 3.

[12] *America's Civic Health Index, Broken Engagement*, A Report by The National Conference on Citizenship in Association with Center for Information and Research on Civic Learning and Engagement (CIRCLE) and Saguaro Seminar (Washington, D.C.: 2006), p. 15.

[13] William Galston, Institute for Philosophy and Public Policy, *Civic Education and Political Participation*, p. 1 (University of Maryland: Undated) ("Some of the basic facts are well known. In the early 1970s, about one half of the 18-29 year olds voted in presidential elections. By 1996, fewer than one-third did. The same pattern holds for congressional elections – about one third in the 1970s, compared to less than one fifth in 1998. Less well known are the trends charted by the remarkable UCLA

study involving 250,000 matriculating college freshmen each year, conducted since the 1960s. Over this period, every significant indicator of political engagement has fallen by at least half"); Karl Kurtz, Alan Rosenthal, and Cliff Zukin, *Citizenship: A Challenge for All Generations,* Representative Democracy in America Project, The National Conference of State Legislatures, Executive Summary (Denver, Colorado: 2003) ("The gap between the civic attitudes, knowledge and participation of the new generation of DotNets and the older ones is substantially greater than the gaps between previous generations. It suggests that the DotNets will never be as engaged in democracy as their elders, even as they age"); *The Civic Mission of Schools,* p. 19 (noting declines in young people's voting, interest in public affairs, and civic knowledge).

[14] *America's Civic Health Index, Broken Engagement,* p. 5.

[15] For an excellent survey regarding this generation's failure to teach and learn American history and civics, see J. Martin Rochester, *The Training of Idiots, Civics Education in America's Schools,* Thomas B. Fordham Foundation, *Where Did Social Studies Go Wrong?* (James Leming, Lucien Ellington, and Kathleen Porter-Magee, eds) (Washington, D.C.: 2003), pp. 6-39.

[16] A. D. Lutkus and A. R. Weiss, U.S. Department of Education, National Center for Education Statistics, *The Nation's Report Card, Civics 2006, National Assessment of Educational Progress at Grades 4, 8, and 12* (Washington, D.C.: 2007), pp. 1, 7.

[17] *Ibid.,* p. 7.

[18] *Ibid.,* p. 71.

[19] J. Lee and A. Weiss, U.S. Department of Education, National Center for Education Statistics, *The Nation's Report Card, U.S. History 2006, National Assessment of Educational Progress at Grades 4, 8, and 12* (Washington, D.C.: 2007), p. 9.

[20] *Ibid.,* p. 1.

[21] Diane Ravitch, National Assessment Governing Board, *Statement Regarding 2001 U.S. History Report Card* (2002).

[22] *Future of the First Amendment,* John S. and James K. Knight Foundation (Miami, Florida: 2005).

[23] Paul Gagnon, *Education Democracy, State Standards to Ensure a Civic Core,* Albert Shanker Institute (Washington, D.C.: 2003), pp. 18-78.

[24] See, *e.g.,* Sheldon Stern, Thomas B. Fordham Institute, *Effective State Standards for U.S. History: A 2003 Report Card* (Washington, D.C.: 2003) (concluding that over three-fifths of state standards possessed weak or ineffective history standards).

[25] *The Civic Missions of Schools,* pp. 14-16; Richard G. Niemi and Julia Smith, *Enrollments in High School Government Classes: Are We Short-Changing Both Citizenship and Political Science Training?,* PS: Political Science & Politics 34 (2001): 281-287; and Nathaniel Leland Schwartz, *Civic Engagement: The Demise of the American High School Civics Class,* Unpublished honors thesis, Harvard University (2002).

[26] See, *e.g.,* Ian Shapira, *More Clout Sought for Social Studies in U.S. Law,* The Washington Post (September 29, 2006), p. BO1.

[27] *Citizenship: A Challenge for All Generations,* Executive Summary.

[28] Michigan Department of Education, Michigan Education Assessment Program Summary Reports (Lansing, Michigan), http://www.michigan. gov/mde and linked

pages (demographic data pursuant to internal Department of Education demographic statistical analysis provided to the author).

[29]Summarizing the results of a statewide poll, Alan B. Bookman, the President of the Florida Bar, for example, concluded that "Floridians score an A on recognizing the importance of the constitutional concepts, but get an F on defining separation of powers and checks and balances, and a D on identifying the three government branches." The Florida State Bar Press Release, *Poll Shows Need for More Civic Education for Florida Adults,* January 11, 2006.

[30]Anne Neal and Jerry Martin, *Losing America's Memory, Historical Illiteracy in the 21st Century,* American Council of Trustees and Alumni (Washington, D.C.: 2000). See also Anne Neal and Jerry Martin, *Restoring America's Legacy,* American Council of Trustees and Alumni (Washington, D.C.: 2002).

[31]*The Coming Crisis in Citizenship, Higher Education's Failure To Teach America's History and Institutions,* Intercollegiate Studies Institute, American Civic Literacy Program (Washington, D.C.: 2006), p. 6.

[32]*Ibid.,* p. 11.

[33]*Democracy at Risk: Renewing the Political Science of Citizenship,* p. 24, citing Michael Delli Carpini and Scott Keeter, *What Americans Know About Politics and Why it Matters* (New Haven: Yale University Press, 1996), p. 196.

[34]*A Plan for the Establishment of Public Schools and the Diffusion of Knowledge in Pennsylvania; to Which Are Added, Thoughts upon the Mode of Education, Proper in a Republic* (1786) (emphasis in original). Rush, therefore, proposed the establishment of public schools so that our youth would become "good citizens of the republic." *Ibid.*

[35]See, *e.g.,* T.L. Pittinsky, S.A. Rosenthal, L.M. Bacon, R.M. Montoya, and W. Zhu, *National Leadership Index 2006: A National Study of Confidence in Leadership, Center for Public Leadership, John F. Kennedy School of Government, Harvard University* (Cambridge, Massachusetts: 2006) (finding that over 70% of Americans believe there is a leadership crisis, especially in the federal government); Edward Carmines, Jessica Gerrity, and Michael Wagner, *How the American Public Views Congress: A Report Based on the Center on Congress' 2004 Public Opinion Survey,* The Center on Congress at Indiana University (2005), pp. 1-2 ("A solid majority, 57 percent of the public, disapproves of the way Congress is doing its job. Only 49 percent of citizens think their congressional representatives have their constituents' interest in mind when voting on policies, while over 63 percent of the public thinks their representative have special interests in mind when casting roll call votes"); Timothy Cook and Paul Gronke, *The Skeptical American: Revisiting the Meanings of Trust in Government and Confidence in Institutions* (2004); Timothy Cook and Paul Gronke, *Trust, Distrust, Confidence, Lack of Confidence: New Evidence of Public Opinion toward Government and Institutions from 2002* (2002).

[36]See, *e.g.,* Constitution of North Carolina, Article XXI (1776).

[37]For a more comprehensive view on this subject, see Michael Warren, *Celebrate U.S. System of Freedom, Equal Rights,* The Detroit News (September, 2002).

[38]For a fuller explanation, see Michael Warren, *Keep 'America' in Michigan Schools, State Bureaucrats Want To Do What Stalin, Osama Could Only Dream About,* The Detroit News (May 24, 2006); *Keep Our Schools Safe for 'Americans,' Michigan Needs To Control Bureaucrats Run Amok,* The Detroit News (May 25, 2006).

Once the effort was exposed, the Superintendent of Public Instruction quashed it. Nevertheless, the effort was seen as so pernicious that the Michigan Legislature felt compelled to act. Section 603 of Michigan Public Act 332 of 2006 (the Michigan Legislature's appropriation bill for the state Department of Education) specifically provided that "The subject area content expectations of social studies shall not prohibit or discourage the use of the word 'American' in referring to a citizen of the United States."

[39]Charles Secondat, Baron de Montesquieu, *The Spirit of the Laws* (1748).

[40]In his *Opening Address to the United Nations General Assembly,* Special Session on Terrorism (October 1, 2001), then Mayor Rudolf Giuliani eloquently explained the motive behind the terrorists who struck his city on September 11, 2001:

> This was not just an attack on the City of New York or on the United States of America. It was an attack on the very idea of a free, inclusive, and civil society. . . .
>
> We are defined as Americans by our beliefs – not by our ethnic origins, our race or our religion. Our beliefs in religious freedom, political freedom, and economic freedom – that's what makes an American. Our belief in democracy, the rule of law, and respect for human life – that's how you become an American. It is these very principles – and the opportunities these principles give to so many to create a better life for themselves and their families – that make America, and New York, a "shining city on a hill." . . .
>
> It is tragic and perverse that it is because of these very principles – particularly our religious, political and economic freedoms – that we find ourselves under attack by terrorists.
>
> Our freedom threatens them, because they know that if our ideas of freedom gain a foothold among their people it will destroy their power. So they strike out against us to keep those ideas from reaching their people.

[41]President Ronald Reagan's warning in his *Farewell Address* (1989) resonates even more powerfully today:

> An informed patriotism is what we want. And are we doing a good enough job teaching our children what America is and what she represents in the long history of the world? Those of us who are over 35 or so years of age grew up in a different America. We were taught, very directly, what it means to be an American. . . .
>
> Younger parents aren't sure that an unambivalent appreciation of America is the right thing to teach modern children. And for

those who create the popular culture, well-grounded patriotism is no longer the style. Our spirit is back, but we haven't reinstitutionalized it. . . .

I'm warning of an eradication of the American memory that could result, ultimately, in an erosion of the American spirit. Let's start with some basics: more attention to American history and a greater emphasis on civic ritual.

[42]See, *e.g.*, J. Martin Rochester, *The Training of Idiots, Civics Education in America's Schools*, pp. 17-26.

[43]*A Dissertation on the Canon and the Feudal Law* (1765).

[44]John Trenchard and Thomas Gordon, authors of a series pamphlets entitled *Cato's Letters*, first published in London during the 1720s, were the most influential Radical Whigs.

[45]*A Dissertation on the Canon and the Feudal Law.*

[46]*Letter to John Adams* (1796).

[47]*Dedication of the Bunker Hill Monument* (1825).

[48]*A Summary View of the Rights of British America* (1774).

[49]*Cato's Letters, No. 25, Considerations on the Destructive Spirit of Arbitrary Power. With the Blessings of Liberty, and Our Own Constitution* (1721).

[50]Thomas Gordon, *Cato's Letters, No. 36, Of Loyalty* (1721).

[51]*Thoughts on Government* (1776).

[52]*Report on the Rights of Colonists, Natural Rights of the Colonists as Men* (Boston, Massachusetts: 1772).

[53]*Fragments of the Discarded First Inaugural Address* (1789).

[54]Washington observed that the rule of law is a profound bar to arbitrary and unjust rule because Congress and the President may not "exempt themselves from consequences of any unjust and tyrannical acts which they impose upon others." *Ibid.*

[55]*Address on Taking the Oath of the Presidency* (1974).

[56]*Report on the Rights of the Colonists.*

[57]*Plessy v Ferguson,* 163 US 537, 559; 16 S Ct 1138 (1896) (Harlan, J., dissenting). The Supreme Court had earlier observed that "The Constitution of the United States is a law for rulers and people, equally in war and in peace, and covers with the shield of its protection all classes of men, at all times, and under all circumstances." *Ex parte Milligan,* 71 US 2, 120-121; 4 Wall 2 (1866).

[58]*Televised Speech* (1962).

[59]*Oration Commemorating the Boston Massacre* (1775).

[60]James Madison, *Federalist Paper No. 48.*

[61]Massachusetts Constitution, Bill of Rights, Article XXX (1780). John Adams was the primary author of the Massachusetts Constitution, and it is the oldest functioning constitution today.

[62]*A Summary View of the Rights of British America.*

[63]See, *e.g.*, Virginia Constitution, Bill of Rights, Section I (1776); Pennsylvania Constitution, Declaration of Rights, Article I (1776) ("all men . . . have certain natural, inherent and

inalienable rights, amongst which are, the enjoying and defending of life and liberty, acquiring, possessing and protecting property, and pursuing and obtaining happiness and safety"); Vermont Constitution, Declaration of Rights, Article I (1777) ("all men ... have certain natural, inherent and unalienable rights, amongst which are, the enjoying and defending of life and liberty, acquiring, possessing and protecting property, and pursuing and obtaining happiness and safety"); Massachusetts Constitution, Bill of Rights, Article I ("All men . . . have certain natural, essential, and unalienable rights, amongst which may be reckoned the right of enjoying and defending their lives and liberty, acquiring, possessing, and protecting property, and pursuing and obtaining happiness and safety"); New Hampshire Constitution, Bill of Rights, Article IV (1784) ("Among the natural rights, some are in their very nature unalienable, because no equivalent can be given or received for them").

[64]For a thorough analysis of these issues – from somewhat different perspectives – see Edmund S. Morgan, *Inventing the People, The Rise of Popular Sovereignty in England and America* (New York, New York: 1988), and R. R. Palmer, *The World of the French Revolution* (New York, New York: 1971).

[65]John Locke, who defined "property" to include freedom of action and liberty in general, explained in detail:

> The supreme power cannot take from any man any part of his property without his own consent. For the preservation of property being the end of government, and that for which men enter into society, it necessarily supposed that requires that the people should have property, without which they must be supposed to lose that by entering into society, which was the end for which they entered into it, too gross an absurdity for any man to own. Men, therefore, in society having property, they have such a right to the goods which by the law of the community are theirs, that nobody hath a right to take them or any part of them from them, without their own consent; without this they have no property at all. For I have truly no property in that which another can by right take from me when he pleases, against my consent. Hence it is a mistake to think that the supreme or legislative power of any commonwealth can do what it will, and dispose of the estates of the subjects arbitrarily, or take any part of them at pleasure. *Second Treatise of Civil Government.*

[66]*Address to the Committee of Correspondence in Barbados* (Philadelphia, Pennsylvania: 1766).
[67]*A Dissertation on the Canon and the Feudal Law.*
[68]Virginia Constitution, Bill of Rights, Section I (1776).
[69]*The Farmer Refuted, or A More Comprehensive and Impartial View of the Disputes Between Great Britain and the Colonies* (New York, New York: 1775).
[70]The English philosophers Thomas Hobbes and John Locke both agreed on this point. Hobbes, for example, wrote:

> THE RIGHT OF NATURE, which writers commonly call *jus naturale*, is the liberty each man hath, to use his owne power, as he

will himself, for the preservation of his own nature; that is to say, of his own life; and consequently, of doing any thing, which in his own judgment, and reason, he shall conceive to be the aptest means thereunto. *Leviathan or the Matter Forme and Power of a Commonwealth Ecclesiasticall and Civil* (1651).

Locke similarly stated that in a state of nature, all men may enforce nature's law: "For in the state of perfect equality, where naturally there is no superiority or jurisdiction of one over another, what may do in prosecution of that law, every one must needs have a right to do." *Second Treatise of Civil Government.*

[71]Virginia Constitution, Bill of Rights, Section I. See also Pennsylvania Constitution, Declaration of Rights, Section I ("all men are born equally free and independent"); Vermont Constitution, Declaration of Rights, Article I ("all men are born equally free and independent"); Massachusetts Constitution, Article I ("All men are born free and equal"); New Hampshire Constitution, Bill of Rights, Article I ("All men are born equally free and independent").

[72]*Second Treatise of Civil Government.*

[73]Locke similarly espied:

He that in the state of nature would take away the freedom that belongs to any one in that state, must necessarily be supposed to have a design to take away everything else, that freedom being the foundation of all the rest; as he that in the state of society would take away the freedom belonging to those of that society or commonwealth, must be supposed to design to take away from them everything else, and so be looked on as in a state of war. *Second Treatise of Civil Government.*

[74]*Ibid.*

[75]*Federalist Paper No. 51.*

[76]*Federalist Paper No. 15.*

[77]*Opening Address to the Pennsylvania Ratifying Convention* (1787).

[78]Massachusetts Constitution, Preamble. See also Delaware Constitution, Declaration of Rights, Section I (1776) ("That all government originates from the people, is founded in compact only, and instituted only for the good of the whole"); Maryland Constitution, Declaration of Rights, Article I (1776) ("That all government of right originates from the people, is founded in compact only, and instituted solely for the good of the whole"); New Hampshire Constitution, Bill of Rights, Article I ("All men are born free and independent; therefore, all government of right originates from the people, is founded in consent, and instituted for the common good").

[79]*The Rights of Man.*

[80]New Hampshire Constitution, Bill of Rights, Article I.

[81]*Leviathan.*

[82]*Letter to Francois D'Ivernois* (1795).

[83]*The Rights of Man.*

[84]*Notes on the State of Virginia.*

[85]*Second Treatise of Civil Government.*

[86]*Letter to James Madison* (1787).

[87]*Report on Public Credit* (1790).

[88]For a modern authority's analysis of how America became a refuge from political persecution and formed new social compacts, see Marilyn Baseler, *"Asylum for Mankind," America 1607-1800* (Ithaca, New York: 1998).

[89]*Democracy in America* (1835).

[90]*Declaration of Causes and Necessity of Taking Up Arms* (1775).

[91]*A Dissertation on the Canon and the Feudal Law.*

[92]*Benjamin Rush Limns Some of the Founding Fathers* (circa 1800).

[93]*Rules for Reducing a Great Empire to a Small One* (1773). Jefferson similarly noted that "America was conquered, and her settlement made and firmly established, at the expense of individuals, and not of the British public. Their own blood was spilt in acquiring lands for their settlement, their own fortunes expended in making that settlement effectual." *A Summary View of the Rights of British America.*

[94]Dr Joseph Warren, *Second Oration Commemorating the Boston Massacre.*

[95]J. Hector St John de Crèvecoeur, *Letter from an American Farmer* (1782).

[96]*Second Oration Commemorating the Boston Massacre.*

[97]*Letter from an American Farmer.*

[98]*Virginia Stamp Act Resolutions* (1765).

[99]*Declaration of The Causes and Necessity of Taking Up Arms* (1775).

[100]In fact, many historians have concluded that the tax structure actually reduced the price of tea to the colonists. See, *e.g.,* Russell Kirk, *Roots of the American Order* (Washington, D.C.: 1991), p. 394; Esmond Wright, *Fabric of Freedom, 1763-1800* (New York, New York: 1964), pp. 67-68.

[101]The Stamp Act Resolutions issued by Virginia's House of Burgesses similarly declared that British attempts to tax in contradiction of the colony's "sole exclusive right and power to lay taxes and impositions upon the inhabitants of this colony . . . has a manifest tendency to destroy British as well as American freedom."

[102]*Instructions of the Town of Braintree Massachusetts on the Stamp Act* (1765).

[103]The First Charter of Virginia (1606), for example, stated that "all and every the Persons being our Subjects . . . shall HAVE and enjoy all Liberties, Franchises, and Immunities, within any of our other Dominions, to all Intents and Purposes, as if they had been abiding and born, within this our Realm of *England,* or any other of our said Dominions." Such rights were also guaranteed in the first Charter of New England (1620), Charter of Massachusetts Bay (1629), Charter of Maryland (1632), Charter of Maine (1639), Charter of Carolina (1662), Charter of Rhode Island (1663), and the Charter of Georgia (1732).

[104]*Letters from a Farmer in Pennsylvania, Letter VII* (1767).

[105]*A Summary View of the Rights of British America.*

[106]*Letter to Bryan Fairfax* (1774).

[107]John Adams protested that this deprivation of the right to trial by jury was more onerous than the Stamp Act's usurpation of taxing authority:

But the most grievous innovation of all, is the alarming extension of the power of courts of admiralty. In these courts, one judge presides alone! No juries have any concern there! The law and the fact are both to be decided by the same single judge, whose commission is only during pleasure, and with whom, as we are told, the most mischievous of all customs has become established, that of taking commissions on all condemnations; so that he is under a pecuniary temptation always against the subject. *Instructions of the Town of Braintree Massachusetts on the Stamp Act.*

[108]*A Summary View of the Rights of British America.*

[109]*Rules for Reducing a Great Empire to a Small One.*

[110]*Letter to the Sheriffs of Bristol* (1777).

[111]*A Summary View of the Rights of British America.* The *Instructions from a Boston Town Meeting to Its Assembly Representatives* (1770) had earlier expressed such sentiments:

> A series of occurrences, many recent events . . . afford great reason to believe that a deep-laid and desperate plan of imperial despotism has been laid, and partly executed, for the extinction of all civil liberty. . . . The august and once revered fortress of English freedom – the admirable work of ages – the BRITISH CONSTITUTION seems fast tottering into fatal and inevitable ruin. The dreadful catastrophe threatens universal havoc, and presents an awful warring to hazard all if, peradventure, we in these distant confines of the earth may prevent being totally overwhelmed and buried under the ruins of our most established rights.

[112]Warren's loss struck hard at the Bostonian revolutionary leaders. Abigail Adams wrote after learning of his death, "My bursting heart must find vent at my pen. I just heard that our dear friend, Dr. Warren, is no more, but fell gloriously fighting for his country; saying, Better to die honorably in the field, than ignominiously upon the gallows. Great is our loss. He has distinguished himself in every engagement, by his courage and fortitude, by animating the soldiers and leading them on by his own example." *Letter to John Adams* (1775).

[113]*Letter of Francis, Lord Rawdon to his Uncle, Francis, Tenth Earl of Huntington* (1775).

[114]*Account [of the Battle of Lexington] by the Provincial Congress at Watertown Massachusetts* (1775).

[115]The last four and half paragraphs of the *Declaration of the Causes and Necessity*, from which the last quotation is derived, were drafted by Jefferson. Although he had drafted a complete *Declaration of the Causes and Necessity*, the Congress approved a second draft, written by Dickinson, which was at the same time both stronger and weaker than Jefferson's – but Dickinson had incorporated Jefferson's last few paragraphs verbatim.

[116]Samuel West, *A Sermon Preached . . . May 29th, 1776, Being the Anniversary for the Election of the Honorable Council for the Colony* (Boston, Massachusetts: 1776).

[117]*Instructions for the Town of Malden, Massachusetts, for a Declaration of Independence* (1776).

[118]*Letter to Abigail Adams* (1776).

[119]Adams explained to Jefferson why Jefferson was required to draft the *Declaration of Independence*: "Reason first – You are a Virginian, and a Virginian ought to appear at

the head of this business. Reason second – I am obnoxious, suspected and unpopular. You are very much otherwise. Reason third – You can write ten times better than I can." *Letter to Timothy Pickering* (1822).

[120]The State of New York abstained.

[121]*Letter to Henry Lee* (1825). John Adams similarly remarked that there was not an idea in the *Declaration of Independence* "but what been hackneyed in the Congress two years before. The substance of it is contained in the *declaration of rights* and the violation of those rights, in the Journals of Congress, 1774." *Letter to Timothy Pickering*.

[122]*Speech to the Second Virginia Convention.*

[123]*A Summary View of the Rights of British America.*

[124]*The Crisis, No. IV* (1777).

[125]*Letter to Thomas Jefferson* (1815).

[126]*Letter to Major John Cartwright* (1824).

[127]Virginia Constitution, Section 1.

[128]Pennsylvania Constitution, Declaration of the Rights, Article 1 ("That all men are born equally free and independent, and have certain natural inherent and inalienable rights, amongst which are, the enjoying and defending life and liberty, acquiring, possessing and protecting property, and pursuing and obtaining happiness and safety"); Delaware Constitution, Declaration of Rights, Article 1, Section 10 ("That all government of right originates from the people, is founded in compact only, and instituted for the good of the whole"; "That every member of society hath a right to be protected in the enjoyment of life, liberty and property"); Maryland Constitution, Article 1 ("That all government of right originates from the people, is founded on compact only, and instituted solely for the good of the whole"); North Carolina Constitution, Declaration of Rights, Article I ("That all political power is vested in and derived from the people only"); Vermont Constitution, Preamble, and Declaration of Rights, Article I ("all government ought to be instituted and supported, for the security and protection of the community, as such, and to enable individuals who compose it, to enjoy their natural rights, and other blessings which the Author of existence has bestowed upon man"; "THAT all men are born free and independent and have certain natural, inherent and unalienable rights, amongst which are the enjoying and defending life and liberty; acquiring, possessing and protecting property, and pursuing and obtaining happiness and safety"); Massachusetts Constitution, Preamble and Declaration of Rights, Article 1 ("The end of the institution, maintenance, and administration of government is to secure the existence of the body politic, to protect it, and to furnish the individuals who compose it with the power of enjoying in safety and tranquility their natural rights, and blessings of life"; "All men are born free and equal, and have certain natural, essential and unalienable rights; among which may be reckoned the right of enjoying and defending their lives and liberties; that of acquiring, possessing, and protecting property; in fine, that of seeking and obtaining safety and happiness"); Constitution of New Hampshire, Articles 1, 2, and 4 ("All men are born equally free and independent; therefore government of right originates from the people, is founded in consent, and instituted for the general good"; "All men have certain natural, essential, and inherent rights; among which are – the enjoying and defending life and liberty – acquiring, possessing and protecting property – and in a word, of seeking and obtaining happiness"; "Among the natural rights, some are in their

very nature unalienable, because no equivalent can be given or received for them").

[129]Virginia Constitution, Bill of Rights, Section I. See also Pennsylvania Constitution, Declaration of Rights, Section 1 ("all men are born equally free and independent"); Vermont Constitution, Declaration of Rights, Article I ("all men are born equally free and independent"); Massachusetts Constitution, Article I ("All men are born free and equal"); New Hampshire Constitution, Bill of Rights, Article I ("All men are born equally free and independent").

[130]Virginia Constitution, Section 1.

[131]New Hampshire Constitution, Articles 3-4.

[132]*Home Building & Loan Association v Blaisdell*, 290 US 398, 454-455; 54 S Ct 231 (1934) (Sutherland, J., dissenting).

[133]*Federalist Paper No. 10.*

[134]*Federalist Paper No. 44.*

[135]For a superb analysis of this worldview, see Gordon S. Wood, *The Radicalism of the American Revolution* (New York, New York: 1993).

[136]*The Defects of the Confederation.*

[137]*Letter to Caleb Davis* (1781).

[138]*Novanglus, or A History of the Dispute with America, From Its Origin, in 1754, to the Present Time, No. 5* (1774).

[139]"Power abused ceases to be lawful authority, and degenerates into tyranny. Liberty abused, or carried to excess, is licentiousness." Henry Cumings, *Sermon Preached May 28, 1783.*

[140]*Pennsylvania Packet* (1786).

[141]*Letter to Abigail Adams.*

[142]Jefferson expressed the prevailing sentiment in a letter: "Doctor Smith, you say, what is the best elementary book on the principles of government? None in the world [is] equal to the Review of Montesquieu. . . ." *Letter to Joseph Cabell* (1816).

[143]*The Spirit of the Laws.*

[144]*Letter to Thomas Jefferson* (1788).

[145]At the same time that the Continental Congress had established a committee to draft the *Declaration of Independence*, it also established a committee to draft a "form of confederation." The draft Articles of Confederation were reported by the committee quickly after the adoption of the *Declaration of Independence*, and the Articles were thereafter referred to the states for ratification. As was symptomatic of governance at the time, the states debated and lingered over the Articles of Confederation for several years. Not until 1781 did the Articles take effect. Nevertheless, Congress apparently acted in accordance with them prior to their ratification. See, *e.g.*, Max Farrand, *The Framing of the Constitution* (New York, New York: 1992 [originally 1913]).

[146]*Comments at the New York Ratifying Convention* (1788).

[147]See, *e.g.*, *Federalist Paper No. 1* ("it will be equally forgotten that the vigor of governments is essential to the security of liberty"); *Federalist Paper No. 26* ("greater energy of government is essential to the welfare and prosperity of the community").

[148]*Federalist Paper No. 21.*

[149]*Autobiography* (1743-1790).

[150]*Ibid.*

[151] *Federalist Paper No. 15.*

[152] An attempt to resolve a dispute between Maryland and Virginia regarding the navigation of the Potomac River led to the Mount Vernon Conference of 1785, followed by the Annapolis Convention in September, 1786. The Annapolis Convention resolved to reconvene in Philadelphia and request the presence of all the States, and Congress authorized the meeting "to take into consideration the trade and commerce of the United States," as well as for examining the defects of the Articles of Confederation and "digesting a plan for supplying such defects as may be discovered to exist." The resolution was drafted by Hamilton.

[153] *Federalist Paper No. 1.*

[154] *Speech before the Virginia Ratifying Convention* (1788).

[155] *Letter to P.S. DuPont de Nemours* (1802).

[156] *Democracy in America.*

[157] *Letter to Dr. Walter Jones* (1814).

[158] *Ibid.*

[159] *Benjamin Rush Limns Some of the Founding Fathers.*

[160] The *Remonstrance* was written to oppose a bill that would have assessed taxes to support teachers of Christianity. Not only was the assessment bill defeated, the following year Virginia enacted a *Statute for Religious Freedom* (1786), based on a bill submitted by Jefferson several years earlier; Madison shepherded the statute through the legislature while Jefferson was in Paris. The arguments set forth in the *Remonstrance* became the underpinning for the *Statute for Religious Freedom*, which, in turn, became the primogenitor for the First Amendment's clauses protecting religious liberty.

[161] *Letter to Jefferson* (1825).

[162] *Letter to Madison* (1788).

[163] *Democracy in America.*

[164] Pennsylvania Constitution, Article IV. See also New Hampshire Constitution, Bill of Rights, Articles V, VII, VIII; Virginia Constitution, Bill of Rights, Section 2 ("That all power is vested in, and consequently derived from, the people; that magistrates are their trustees and servants, and at all times amenable to them"); North Carolina Constitution, Article I ("That all political power is vested in and derived from the people only"); Vermont Constitution, Article V ("That all power being originally inherent in, and consequently, derived from the people; therefore, all officers of government, whether legislative or executive, are their trustees and servants, and at all times accountable to them").

[165] *Federalist Paper No. 22.*

[166] *Ibid.*

[167] *Speech before the Virginia Ratifying Convention.*

[168] *Federalist Paper No. 46.* Senator Daniel Webster echoed this understanding decades later on the Senate floor:

> Is [the federal government] the creature of the State legislatures, or the creature of the people? . . . It is, Sire, the people's government, made for the people, made by the people, and answerable to the people. . . . I hold it to be a popular government, erected by the

people; those who administer it responsible to the people; and itself capable of being amended and modified, just as the people may choose it should be. . . . We are here to administer a Constitution emanating immediately from the people, and trusted by them to our administration. It is not the creature of the State governments. *Reply to Hayne* (1830).

[169]Maryland Constitution, Declaration of Rights, Article IV. See also Delaware Constitution, Declaration of Rights, Article 6 ("the right in the people to participate in the Legislature, is the foundation of liberty and of all free government, and for this end all elections ought to be free and frequent, and every freeman, having sufficient evidence of a permanent common interest with, and attachment to the community, hath a right to suffrage").

[170]*Letter to Mayor William Hunter* (1790).

[171]*Federalist Paper No. 3.*

[172]*Federalist Paper No. 10.*

[173]*Federalist Paper No. 1.*

[174]*Letter to Thomas Nelson* (1776).

[175]*Federalist Paper No. 51.* Madison similarly remarked at the Convention:

In order to judge of the form to be given to this institution, it will be proper to take a view of the ends to be served by it. These were, first, to protect the people against their rulers; secondly, to protect the people against the transient impressions into which they themselves might be led.

[176]*Federalist Paper No. 51.*

[177]*Federalist Paper No. 47.* Madison made similar remarks at the Convention:

If it be a fundamental principle of free government that the legislative, executive, and judiciary powers should be separately exercised, it is equally so that they be independently exercised. . . .

If it be essential to the preservation of liberty that the legislative, executive, and judiciary powers be separate, it is essential to a maintenance of the separation that they should be independent of each other. . . . [A] dependence of the executive on the legislature would render it the executor as well as the maker of laws, and then, according to the observation of Montesquieu, tyrannical laws may be made that they may be executed in a tyrannical manner.

[178]*The Spirit of the Laws.*

[179]*Ibid.*

[180]*Federalist Paper No. 47.*

[181]*Federalist Paper No. 48.*

[182]He continued in *Federalist Paper No. 5*:

But the great security against a gradual concentration of the several powers in the same department consists in giving to those who administer each department the necessary constitutional means and personal motives to resist encroachments of the others. The provision for defense must in this, as in all other cases, be made commensurate to the danger of attack. Ambition must be made to counteract ambition.

Hamilton agreed that "This partial intermixture is even, in some cases, not only proper but necessary to the mutual defense of the several members of the government against each other." *Federalist Paper No. 66.*

[183]Internal checks related to the Supreme Court include the "case and controversy" limit on its jurisdiction – *i.e.,* the Court may not issue declaratory rulings, may only decide cases involving real disputes and parties which have been submitted to the courts that have not been rendered moot, and, except in very limited circumstances, only renders decisions on cases that have been appealed to the Court. In addition, the Court must publish decisions and follow precedent. The major internal check involving the President is the two-term limit.

[184]*Thoughts on Government.*

[185]Madison similarly illustrated in *Federalist Paper No. 51:*

> In republican government, the legislative authority necessarily predominates. The remedy for this inconvenience is to divide the legislature into different branches; and to render them, by different modes of election and different principles of action, as little connected with each other as the nature of their common functions and their common dependence on the society will admit.

[186]"This power over the purse may, in fact, be regarded as the most complete and effectual weapon with which any constitution can arm the immediate representatives of the people, for obtaining a redress of every grievance, and for carrying into effect every just and salutary measure." Madison, *Federalist Paper No. 53.*

[187]*Thoughts on Government.* James Wilson expressed a similar sentiment at the Convention regarding the Legislative branch in general:

> The government ought to possess not only, first, the force, but second, the mind or sense of the people at large. The legislature ought to be the most exact transcript of the whole society. Representation is made necessary only because it is impossible for the people to act collectively.

[188]*Federalist Paper No. 62.*

[189]Farrand, *The Framing of the Constitution,* p. 74.

[190]*Federalist Paper No. 78.*

[191]*Ibid.*

[192]*Ibid.*

[193]*Ibid.* "Nor does this conclusion by any means suppose a superiority of the judicial to the legislative power. It only supposes that the power of the people is superior to both,

and that where the will of the legislature, declared in its statutes, stands in opposition to that of the people, declared in the Constitution, the judges ought to be governed by the latter rather than the former." *Ibid.*

[194]*Ibid.*

[195]*Democracy in America.* Several generations later, when faced with President Franklin D. Roosevelt's scheme to "pack" the Supreme Court with several additional Justices – with the clear intent of creating a majority that would approve the New Deal's legislative agenda – the Senate Judiciary Committee reaffirmed America's deep seated commitment to independent judicial review:

> Shall we now, after 150 years of loyalty to the constitutional ideal of an untrammeled judiciary, duty bound to protect the constitutional rights of the humblest citizen even against the Government itself, create the vicious precedent which must necessarily undermine our system? . . .

> This amounts to nothing more than the declaration that when the Court stands in the way of a legislative enactment, the Congress may reverse the ruling by enlarging the Court. When such a principle is adopted, our constitutional system is overthrown! . . . .

> Let us now . . . declare that we would rather have an independent Court, a fearless Court, a Court that would dare to announce its honest opinions in what it believes to be the defense of the liberties of the people, than a Court that, out of fear or sense of obligation to the appointing power, or factional passion, approves any measure we may enact. We are not the judges of the judges. We are not above the Constitution. *Report of the Committee on the Judiciary,* United States Senate (June 7, 1937).

[196]*Letter of Samuel Adams to James Warren* (1775).

[197]Article 1, Section 9: "The privilege of the writ of habeas corpus shall not be suspended, unless in cases of rebellion or invasion the public safety may require it. No bill of attainder or ex post facto law shall be passed."

[198]*Letter to James Madison* (1787). Another member of the Founding Generation, in the course of expressing dismay at the glaring exclusion, explained that "Bills of Rights have been the happy instruments of wresting the privileges and rights of the people from the hand of Despotism. . . . Bills of Rights, in my opinion, are the grand bulwarks of freedom." *Letter of Thomas B. Wait to George Thatcher* (1788).

[199]*Speech before the Virginia Ratifying Convention.*

[200]*Ibid.*

[201]Delegate Theophilus Parsons of Massachusetts remarked at the Massachusetts Ratification Convention that "No power was given to Congress to infringe on any one of the natural rights of the people by this Constitution; and, should they attempt it without constitutional authority, the act would be a nullity and could not be enforced."

Debates in the Convention of the Commonwealth of Massachusetts on the Adoption of the Federal Constitution (1788).

[202] *Federalist Paper No. 84.*

[203] The concept of a Bill of Rights originated from England with the adoption of the *Magna Carta* in 1215. The great charter established the principle that no taxation should occur without representation, guaranteed a trial by a jury of one's peers, and made due process the law of the land. Originally established to protect the nobility from the oppression of the King, this original protection of English liberty was subsequently expanded through a series of written and binding enactments of King and Parliament. The *Confirmato Cartarum* (1297), *Petition of Right* (1628), *Habeas Corpus Act* (1679), and *Bill of Rights* (1689) all confirmed or expanded the rights of Englishmen.

[204] The Eleventh Amendment was ratified over 200 years later. The final amendment proposed by Madison to be ratified – the long delayed Twenty-Seventh Amendment – prohibits Congress from receiving a pay increase until after the election following its approval.

[205] *The Blessings of Liberty, Address at the Second Century Convocation of Washington University.*

[206] *Ex parte Milligan,* 71 US at 120.

[207] *West Virginia State Board of Education v Barnette,* 319 US 624, 639; 63 S Ct 1178 (1943).

[208] Hamilton, *Federalist Paper No. 81.*

[209] *Federalist Paper No. 10.* As Madison had earlier stated before the Convention: "The lesson we are to draw from the whole is that where a majority are united by a common sentiment and have an opportunity, the rights of the minor party become insecure. In a republican government, the majority, if united, have always an opportunity."

[210] Madison explained:

> The diversity in the faculties of men, from which the rights of property originate, is not less an insuperable obstacle to a uniformity of interests. The protection of these faculties is the first object of government. From the protection of different and unequal faculties of acquiring property, the possession of different degrees and kinds of property immediately results; and from the influence of these on the sentiments and views of the respective proprietors ensues a division of society into different interests and parties. *Federalist Paper No. 10.*

[211] Madison elaborated in *Federalist Paper No. 10*:

> There are two methods of curing the mischiefs of faction: the one, by removing its causes; the other, by controlling its effects.

> There are again two methods of removing the causes of faction: the one, by destroying the liberty which is essential to its existence; the other, by giving to every citizen the same opinions, the same passions, and the same interests.

> It could never be more truly said than of the first remedy that it

was worse than the disease. Liberty is to faction what air is to fire, an aliment without which it instantly expires. But it could not be a less folly to abolish liberty, which is essential to political life, because it nourishes faction than it would be to wish the annihilation of air, which is essential to animal life, because it imparts to fire its destructive agency.

The second expedient is as impracticable as the first would be unwise. As long as the reason of man continues fallible, and he is at liberty to exercise it, different opinions will be formed.

[212]Madison detailed his concern:

[A] body of men are unfit to be both judges and parties at the same time; yet what are many of the most important acts of legislation but so many judicial determinations, not indeed concerning the rights of single persons, but concerning the rights of large bodies of citizens? And what are the different classes of legislators but advocates and parties to the causes to which they determine? . . . Yet the parties are, and must be, themselves judges; and the most numerous party, or in other words, the most powerful faction must be expected to prevail. *Ibid.*

[213]Madison's theory was also diametrically opposed to the approach posited by key Jacobin leaders of the French Revolution. Antoine Louis Léon de Richebourg de Saint-Just, for example, denounced factions in startling terms before the National Convention in 1794:

Every party is criminal, for it is a form of isolation from the people and the popular societies, a form of independence from the government. Every faction is criminal because it tends to divide the citizens; every faction is criminal because it neutralizes the power of public virtue; . . . The sovereignty of the people demands that the people be unified; it is therefore opposed to factions, and all faction is a criminal attack upon sovereignty.

This extremist view was one of the underlying reasons for the purges, arrests, and executions of various French political activists and leaders during the French Revolution – eventually including Saint-Just and several of his colleagues on the Committee for Public Society, such as Maximilien Francois Marie Isadore Robespierre.

[214]*Federalist Paper No. 32.*
[215]*Federalist Paper No. 39.*
[216]*Ibid.*
[217]*Federalist Paper No. 83.*
[218]*Federalist Paper No. 45.*
[219]*Essay No. I* (1787).
[220]*Federalist Paper No. 41.*

[221] *Opinion on the Constitutionality of the Bank* (1791).

[222] *Veto of the Bonus Bill* (1817).

[223] *Ibid.*

[224] *Ibid.*

[225] *Veto of Cumberland Road Bill* (1822).

[226] *Federalist Paper No. 40.*

[227] *Federalist Paper No. 46.*

[228] *Federalist Paper No. 45.*

[229] *Federalist Paper No. 51.*

[230] *Letter to A.L.C. Destutt de Tracy* (1811). Jefferson later elaborated in another letter:

> No, my friend, the way to have good and safe government, is not to trust it all to one, but to divide it among the many, distributing to every one exactly the functions he is competent to. Let the national government be entrusted with the defence of the nation, and its foreign and federal relations; the State governments with the civil rights, laws, police, and administration of what concerns the State generally. . . . What has destroyed liberty and the rights of man in every government which has ever existed under the sun? The generalizing and concentrating of all cares and powers into one body. . . . *Letter to Joseph Cabell* (1816).

[231] *Federalist Paper No. 61.*

[232] *Federalist Paper No. 17.*

[235] *Federalist Paper No. 28.*

[234] *Brutus, Essay No. I.*

[235] *Autobiography* (emphasis in original).

[236] The differences between the French Revolution and the American are again highlighted by the differing approaches to local authority. The French made federalism a criminal offense punishable by death.

[237] *Letter to David Humphreys* (1789).

[238] *Letter to Dr Joseph Priestley* (1801).

[239] One purposeful omission from this work, for example, is the struggle for racial equality by Asians – most especially Japanese and Chinese.

[240] *Letters from a Farmer in Pennsylvania, Letter VII.*

[241] *Novanglus, or A History of the Dispute with America, From Its Origin, in 1754, to the Present Time, No. 2.*

[242] *Notes on the State of Virginia.*

[243] *Walker's Appeal in Four Articles, Together with a Preamble to the Coloured Citizens of the World, but in Particular and Very Expressly to Those of the United States of America* (1829).

[244] *Ibid.*

[245] *Independence Day Speech at Rochester* (1852).

[246] *The Watchman's Alarm to Lord N--h. . . .* (Salem, Massachusetts: 1774).

[247] *Address to the Inhabitants of the British Settlements, on the Slavery of the Negroes in America* (1773).

[248] *Draft of the Declaration of Independence* (1776).

[249] *Oration of Advantages of American Independence* (1778). See also generally, Gordon S. Wood, *The Radicalism of the American Revolution.*

[250] *The Slaves' Appeal to the Royal Governor of Massachusetts* (1774) (spelling errors corrected).

[251] *An Address to the Slaves of the United States of America (a/k/a Call to Rebellion), Address to the National Negro Convention at Buffalo, New York* (1843).

[252] *Independence Day Speech at Rochester.*

[253] *Ibid.*

[254] *An Address to the Slaves of the United States of America (a/k/a Call to Rebellion), Address to the National Negro Convention at Buffalo.*

[255] *Dred Scott v Sanford,* 60 US (19 How) 393 (1857).

[256] *Notes on the State of Virginia.*

[257] *Speech on the Dred Scott Decision at Springfield, Illinois* (1857).

[258] *Speech on the Kansas-Nebraska Act at Peoria, Illinois* (1854).

[259] See, *e.g., Black Code of Mississippi* (1865).

[260] *Eulogy of Hon. Charles Sumner* (1865).

[261] *Speech at the National Convention of Colored Men at Louisville, Kentucky* (1883).

[262] *Ibid.*

[263] *Address to the American Missionary Association* (1894).

[264] 83 US (16 Wall) 36 (1872).

[265] 83 US at 78.

[266] 109 US 3; 3 S Ct 18 (1883).

[267] Justice Harlan's dissent reasoned:

> It is expressly conceded by [the majority of the Court] that the thirteenth amendment established freedom; that there are burdens and disabilities, the necessary incidents of slavery, which constitute its substance and visible form; that congress, by the act of 1866, passed in view of the thirteenth amendment, before the fourteenth was adopted, undertook to remove certain burdens and disabilities, the necessary incidents of slavery, and to secure to all citizens of every race and color, and without regard to previous servitude, those fundamental rights which are the essence of civil freedom, namely, the right to make and enforce contracts, to sue, be parties, give evidence, and to inherit, purchase, lease, sell, and convey property as is enjoyed by white citizens; that under the thirteenth amendment congress has to do with slavery and its incidents; and that legislation, so far as necessary or proper to eradicate all forms and incidents of slavery and involuntary servitude, may be direct and primary, operating upon the acts of individuals, whether sanctioned by state legislation or not. These propositions conceded, it is impossible, as it seems to me, to question the constitutional validity of the civil rights act of 1866. . . . Congress, therefore, under its express power to enforce that amendment, by appropriate legislation, may enact laws to protect that people against the deprivation, *on account of their*

race, of any civil rights enjoyed by other freemen of the same state.
. . . *Id.* at 35-36.
[268]163 US 537; 16 S Ct 1138 (1896).
[269]*Id.* at 555. He elaborated:

> They had, as this court has said, a common purpose, namely to
> secure "to a race recently emancipated, a race that through many
> generations have been held in slavery, all the civil rights that the
> superior race enjoy." They declared, in legal effect, this court further
> said, "that the law in the states shall be the same for the black as
> for the white, shall stand equal before the laws of the states; and
> in regard to the colored race, for whose protection the amendment
> was primarily designed, that no discrimination shall be made against
> them by law because of their color." *Id.* at 555-556.

Harlan also found that the amendments forbid "so far as civil and political rights are
concerned, discrimination by the general government or the states against any citizen
because of his race. All citizens are equal before the law." *Id.* at 556, *quoting Gibson v State*,
162 US 565; 16 S Ct 904 (1896).
[270]163 US at 557. Yet, Harlan continued, "If a white man and a black man choose to
occupy the same public conveyance on a public highway, it is their right to do so; and no
government, proceeding alone on grounds of race, can prevent it without infringing the
personal liberty of each." *Id.*
[271]*Id.* at 559-561.
[272]Cong, Globe, 1st Sess, 39th Congress, part 1, p. 474 (1866).
[273]163 US at 543.
[274]*I Have a Dream* (1963).
[275]347 US 483; 74 S Ct 686 (1954).
[276]*Id.* at 494.
[277]379 US 241; 85 S Ct 348 (1964).
[278]379 US 294; 85 S Ct 377 (1964).
[279]*McLaughlin v Florida*, 379 US 184; 85 S Ct 283 (1964).
[280]*Loving v Virginia*, 388 US 1; 87 S Ct 1817 (1967).
[281]*Letter from Birmingham City Jail* (1963).
[282]*I Have a Dream.*
[283]*Letter to John Adams* (1776).
[284]*Letter to Abigail Adams* (1776).
[285]*Seneca Falls Declaration of Sentiments and Resolutions.*
[286]*Letter to Mary S. Parker* (1837). Parker was the President of the Boston Female Anti-
Slavery Society.
[287]*Bradwell v Illinois*, 83 US (16 Wall) 130, 141 (1872) (Bradley, concurring).
[288]*Letter to Mary S. Parker.*
[289]*Ibid.*
[290]*Address to the New York State Legislature* (1860).
[291]*Ibid.*

[292]*Women's Right to Vote* (1873).

[293]*Ibid.*

[294]*Ibid.*

[295]*Ibid.*

[296]*Ibid.*

[297]*The Solitude of Self* (1892).

[298]*Address to the New York State Legislature* (1860).

[299]*Ibid.*

[300]*Ibid.*

[301]*The Solitude of Self.*

[302]*Ibid.*

[303]*Address to the New York State Legislature* (1860).

[304]*Letter to Mary S. Parker.*

[305]See, *e.g., Craig v Boren,* 429 US 190; 97 S Ct 451 (1976).

[306]*The Blessings of Liberty, Address at the Second Century Convocation of Washington University* (1955).

[307]*An Examination into the Leading Principles of the Federal Constitution* (Philadelphia, Pennsylvania: 1787).

[308]*The Blessings of Liberty, Address at the Second Century Convocation of Washington University.*

[309]*Selma Voting Rights March Commemoration* (March, 2007).

[310]For a policy adopting this approach, see *Policy on Learning Expectations for Michigan Students,* Michigan State Board of Education (Lansing, Michigan: 2002).

[311]For comprehensive reviews and policy recommendations regarding this perspective, see *Embracing the Information Age,* Michigan State Board of Education, Task Force Report (Michael David Warren, Jr, Chair) (Lansing, Michigan: 2001); *Any Time, Any Place, Any Path, Any Pace, Taking the Lead on e-Learning Policy,* National Association of State Boards of Education's Report on e-Learning (Washington, D.C: 2001); and Thomas Watkins, *Exploring E-Learning Reforms for Michigan, The New Education (R)evolution* (Detroit, Michigan: 2005), http://www.coe.wayne.edu/elearningReport.pdf.

[312]See, *e.g.,* Chester Finn, Jr, Thomas B. Fordham Foundation, *Where Did Social Studies Go Wrong?,* pp. iii-v.

[313]*Letter to James Warren* (1774).

[314]*The Coming Crisis in Citizenship, Higher Education's Failure To Teach America's History and Institutions,* pp. 8, 22.

[315]*Ibid.,* p. 16.

[316]See, *e.g.,* Margaret A. Nash, *"How to Be Thankful for Being Free": Searching for a Convergence of Discourses on Teaching Patriotism, Citizenship, and United States History,* Teachers College Record, Volume 107, Number 1 (2005), pp. 214-240 (documenting the failure to grasp key historical dates, figures, and philosophical concepts by teacher credential candidates at a large urban Midwestern university); Diane Ravitch, *A Brief History of Social Studies, Where Did Social Studies Go Wrong?,* pp. 1-5 (explaining how modern social studies teacher preparation institutions have devalued the importance of historical events and figures).

[317]*Response to an Address by the President of the United States at the John Marshall Bicentennial*

Ceremonies of the American Bar Association (1955).

[318]*Debate in the House of Commons* (1775).

[319]*Speech at Chicago, Illinois*.

[320]*Letter to Abigail Adams* (1776).

[321]*Address at the Justice Louis Dembitz Brandeis Centennial Convocation of Brandeis University* (1956).

[322]*Letter to Edward Carrington* (1787).

[323]Joceyln Noveck, *AP Tries Ban to Find Out If We Need Paris*, The Oakland Press (March, 2007).

[324]A note of fair disclosure – the author is a member of the Board of Directors of the Michigan Center for Civic Education.

[325]Pennsylvania Constitution, Declaration of Rights, Article XIV.

[326]Vermont Constitution, Declaration of Rights, Article XVI ("That frequent recurrence to fundamental principles, and a firm adherence to justice, moderation, temperance, industry and frugality, are absolutely necessary to preserve the blessings of government, and keep government free. The people ought, therefore, to pay particular attention to these points, in the choice of officers and representatives, and have a right to exact a due and constant regard to them, from their legislators and magistrates, in the making and executing such laws as are necessary for the good government of the State"); Massachusetts Constitution, Bill of Rights, Article XVIII ("A frequent recurrence to the fundamental principles of the constitution, and a constant adherence to those of piety, justice, moderation, temperance, industry and frugality, are absolutely necessary to preserve the advantages of liberty, and to maintain a free government. The people ought, consequently, to have a particular attention to all those principles, in the choice of their officers and representatives: and they have a right to require of their lawgivers and magistrates an exact and constant observance of them, in the formation and execution of the laws necessary for the good administration of the commonwealth"); New Hampshire Constitution, Bill of Rights, Article XXXVIII ("A frequent recurrence to the fundamental principles of the Constitution, and a constant adherence to justice, moderation, temperance, industry, frugality, and all the social virtues, are indispensably necessary to preserve the blessings of liberty and good government; the people ought, therefore, to have a particular regard to all those principles in the choice of their officers and representatives: and they have a right to require of their law-givers and magistrates, an exact and constant observance of them in the formation and execution of the laws necessary for the good administration of government").

[327]*A Plan for the Establishment of Public Schools and the Diffusion of Knowledge in Pennsylvania; to Which Are Added, Thoughts upon the Mode of Education, Proper in a Republic*.

[328]*First Inaugural Address* (1801).

Select Bibliography

Adams, John. *The Political Writings of John Adams* (George Peek, Jr, ed) (New York, New York: 1954)

Adams, John. *The Revolutionary Writings of John Adams* (C. Bradley Thompson, ed) (Indianapolis, Indiana: 2000)

Albert Shanker Institute. *Education for Democracy* (Washington, D.C.: 2003)

American Bar Association; Harris Interactive Market Research Report. *Civics Education* (Chicago, Illinois: 2005)

American Government, Readings and Documents (Peter H. Odegard, ed) (New York, New York: 1966)

American Historical Documents (Harold Syrett, ed) (New York, New York: 1963)

American Historical Documents, 1000-1904 (Danbury, Connecticut: 1991)

American Patriotism, Speeches, Letters, and Other Papers Which Illustrate The Foundation, The Development, The Preservation of the United States of America (Selim Peabody, ed) (New York, New York: 1880)

American Political Science Association Standing Committee on Civic Education and Engagement. *Democracy at Risk: Renewing the Political Science of Citizenship, Final Draft for Review presented at Annual Meeting of the American Political Science Association* (Chicago, Illinois: 2004)

American Political Writing During the Founding Era 1760-1805 (Charles Hyneman and Donald Lutz, eds) (Indianapolis, Indiana: 1983)

An American Primer (Daniel Boorstin, ed) (Chicago, Illinois: 1966)

The American Reader, Words that Moved a Nation (Diane Ravitch, ed) (New York, New York: 1991)

www.americanrhetoric.com

The Anti-Federalists and the Constitutional Convention Debates (Ralph Ketcham, ed) (New York, New York: 1986)

Bailyn, Bernard. *The Ideological Origins of the American Revolution (Enlarged Edition)*

(Cambridge, Massachusetts: 1992)

Baker, Daniel. *Power Quotes* (Detroit, Michigan: 1992)

Baseler, Marilyn. *"Asylum for Mankind," America 1607-1800* (Ithaca, New York: 1998)

Black Protest Thought in the Twentieth Century (2nd Edition) (August Meir, Elliot Rudwick, and Francis Broderick, eds) (Indianapolis, Indiana: 1971)

Bowen, Catherine Drinker. *Miracle at Philadelphia, The Story of the Constitutional Convention, May to September 1787* (New York, New York: 1986)

Breyer, Stephen. *Active Liberty, Interpreting Our Democratic Constitution* (New York, New York: 2005)

Brookhiser, Richard. *Founding Father, Rediscovering George Washington* (New York, New York: 1996)

Bury, J. B. *A History of Freedom of Thought* (New York, New York: 1913)

Carmines, Edward; Gerrity, Jessica; and Wagner, Michael; The Center on Congress at Indiana University. *How the American Public Views Congress: A Report Based on the Center on Congress' 2004 Public Opinion Survey* (2005)

Carnegie Corporation of New York and The Center for Information and Research on Civic Learning and Engagement (CIRCLE). *The Civic Mission of Schools* (New York, New York: 2003)

Centennial Offering, Republication of Principles and Acts of the Revolution in America (Hezekiah Niles, ed) (New York, New York: 1876)

Cheney, Lynne. *A Time for Freedom* (New York, New York: 2005)

Chinard, Gilbert. *Thomas Jefferson: The Apostle of Americanism* (Ann Arbor, Michigan: 1962)

Connelly, Owen. *French Revolution/Napoleonic Era* (New York, New York: 1979)

Cook, Timothy and Gronke, Paul. *The Skeptical American: Revisiting the Meanings of Trust in Government and Confidence in Institutions* (2004)

Cook, Timothy and Gronke, Paul. *Trust, Distrust, Confidence, Lack of Confidence: New Evidence of Public Opinion toward Government and Institutions from 2002* (2002)

Crèvecoeur, J. Hector St. John de. *Letters from an American Farmer and Sketches of Eighteen-Century America* (Albert Stone, ed) (New York, New York: 1986 (originally published in 1782 and 1925))

Cunningham, Jr, Noble. *In the Pursuit of Reason, The Life of Thomas Jefferson* (New

York, New York: 1987)

Davis, David Brion. *Slavery and Human Progress* (Oxford, England: 1984)

The Debate on the American Revolution, 1761-1783, A Sourcebook (Max Beloff, ed) (New York, New York: 1960)

Debate on the Constitution (Bernard Bailyn, ed) (New York, New York: 1993)

The Debates in the Several State Constitutions on the Adoption of the Federal Constitution as Recommended by the General Convention at Philadelphia in 1787 (Jonathan Elliot, ed)

The Democracy Reader, Classic and Modern Speeches, Essays, Poems, Declarations and Documents on Freedom and Human Rights Worldwide (Diane Ravitch & Abigail Thernstrom, eds) (New York, New York: 1992)

Dickinson, John. *Letters from a Farmer in Pennsylvania* (The On-Line Library of Liberty: 2004 (originally published 1767))

A Documentary History of the United States (50th Anniversary Edition) (Richard Heffner, ed) (New York, New York: 2002)

Documents of American History Volume I (5th Edition) (Henry Steele Commager, ed) (New York, New York: 1949)

Evans, Sara. *Born for Liberty, A History of Women in America* (New York, New York: 1989)

Farkas, Steve; Johnson, Jean; and Duffett, Ann; Public Agenda for the National Constitution Center. *Knowing it By Heart, Americans Consider the Constitution and its Meaning* (Philadelphia, Pennsylvania: 2002)

Farrand, Max. *The Framing of the Constitution* (New York, New York: 1992 (originally published 1913))

Feminism: The Essential Historical Writings (Miriam Schneir, ed) (New York, New York: 1992)

Fischer, David Hackett. *Liberty and Freedom, A Visual History of America's Founding Ideas* (New York, New York: 2005)

Fleming, Thomas. *Liberty! The American Revolution* (New York, New York: 1997)

Foner, Eric. *Nothing But Freedom, Emancipation and Its Legacy* (Baton Rouge, Louisana: 1983)

Foner, Eric. *Reconstruction, America's Unfinished Revolution, 1863-1877* (New York, New York: 1989)

Foner, Eric. *The Story of American Freedom* (New York, New York: 1998)

Franklin, Benjamin. *The Autobiography and Selections from His Other Writings* (Herbert Schneider, ed) (Indianapolis, Indiana: 1952)

Franklin, Benjamin. *Writings* (J.A. Leo Lemay, ed) (New York, New York: 1987)

Freedom, Quotes and Passages from the World's Greatest Freethinkers (Leonard Frank, ed) (New York, New York: 2003)

Freeman, Douglas Southall. *Washington, An Abridgment by Richard Harwell of the Pulitzer Prize-Winning Seven-Volume George Washington* (New York, New York: 1968)

Friedan, Betty. *The Feminine Mystique* (New York, New York: 1963)

Frothingham, Richard. *Life and Times of Joseph Warren* (Boston, Massachusetts: 1865)

Gagnon, Paul; Albert Shanker Institute. *Education Democracy, State Standards to Ensure a Civic Core* (Washington, D.C.: 2003)

Galston, William; Institute for Philosophy and Public Policy. *Civic Education and Political Participation* (University of Maryland: Undated)

Gaustad, Edwin. *Sworn on the Altar of God, A Religious Biography of Thomas Jefferson* (Grand Rapids, Michigan: 1996)

Gossett, Thomas. *Race, The History of an Idea in America* (New York, New York: 1965)

Hamilton, Alexander; Madison, James; and Jay, John. *The Federalist Papers* (Isaac Kramnick, ed) (New York, New York: 1987 (originally published 1788))

Hobbes, Thomas. *Leviathan or the Matter Forme and Power of a Commonwealth Ecclesiasticall and Civil* (Michael Oakeshott, ed) (New York, New York: 1962 (originally published 1651))

The Inaugural Addresses of the Presidents (John Hunt, ed) (New York, New York: 1995)

Intercollegiate Studies Institute; American Civic Literacy Program. *The Coming Crisis in Citizenship, Higher Education's Failure To Teach America's History and Institutions* (Washington, D.C.: 2006)

Jefferson, Thomas. *The Thomas Jefferson Papers* (Frank Donovan, ed) (New York, New York: 1963)

Jefferson, Thomas. *Thomas Jefferson, Writings* (Merrill D. Peterson, ed) (New York, New York: 1984)

John S. and James K. Knight Foundation. *Future of the First Amendment* (Miami, Florida: 2005)

Keep Our Schools Safe for 'Americans,' Michigan Needs to Control Bureaucrats Run Amok, The Detroit News (May 25, 2006)

Ketcham, Ralph. *James Madison, A Biography* (Charlottesville: University of Virginia Press: 1990)

Kirk, Russell. *Roots of the American Order* (Washington, D.C.: 1991)

Kraditor, Aileen. *The Ideas of the Woman Suffrage Movement/1890-1920* (New York, New York: 1981)

Kurtz, Karl; Rosenthal, Alan; and Zukin, Cliff; The National Conference of State Legislatures Representative Democracy in America Project. *Citizenship: A Challenge for All Generations* (Denver, Colorado: 2003)

Langguth, Al J. *Patriots: The Men Who Started the American Revolution* (New York, New York: 1988)

Lee, J. and Weiss, A.; U.S. Department of Education, National Center for Education Statistics. *The Nation's Report Card, U.S. History 2006, National Assessment of Educational Progress at Grades 4, 8, and 12* (Washington, D.C.: 2007)

Letters of Delegates to Congress, 1774-1789, Vol II (Paul Smith et al, eds) (Washington, D.C.: 1976-2000)

Letters of a Nation, A Collection of Extraordinary American Letters (Andrew Carroll, ed) (New York, New York: 1997)

Lincoln, Abraham. *The Essential Lincoln* (John Gabriel Hunt, ed) (New York, New York: 1993)

Lincoln, Abraham. *Lincoln, Speeches and Writings 1832-1858* (Don Fehrenbacher, ed) (New York, New York: 1989)

Living History America, The History of the United States in Documents, Essays, Letters, Songs and Poems (Erik Bruun and Jay Crosby, eds) (New York, New York: 1999)

Locke, John. *Second Treatise of Civil Government* (Chicago, Illinois: 1971 (originally published in 1689))

Lutkus, A. D. and Weiss, A. R.; U.S. Department of Education, National Center for Education Statistics. *The Nation's Report Card, Civics 2006, National*

Assessment of Educational Progress at Grades 4, 8, and 12 (Washington, D.C.: 2007)

Maier, Pauline. *American Scripture, Making the Declaration of Independence* (New York, New York: 1997)

Matthews, Richard. *The Radical Politics of Thomas Jefferson, A Revisionist View* (Lawrence, Kansas: 1986)

McCormick Tribune Freedom Museum. *Americans' Awareness of First Amendment Freedoms* (Chicago, Illinois: 2006)

McCullough, David. *1776* (New York, New York: 2005)

McDonald, Forrest. *Alexander Hamilton, A Biography* (New York, New York: 1982)

Memorial of Abraham Lincoln, Late President of the United States (Boston, Massachusetts: 1865)

Michigan Department of Education, *Michigan Education Assessment Program Summary Reports* (Lansing, Michigan)

Michigan State Board of Education; Embracing the Information Age Task Force. *Embracing the Information Age* (Michael David Warren, Jr, Chair) (Lansing, Michigan: 2001)

Michigan State Board of Education. *Policy on Learning Expectations for Michigan Students* (Lansing, Michigan: 2002)

Montesquieu, Charles Secondat, Baron de. *The Spirit of the Laws* (translated by Thomas Nugent) (New York, New York: 1965 (originally published in 1748))

Morgan, Edmund S. *The Birth of the Republic, 1763-89 (3rd Edition)* (Chicago, Illinois: 1992)

Morgan, Edmund S. *Inventing the People, The Rise of Popular Sovereignty in England and America* (New York, New York: 1988)

Murphy, Paul. *World War I and the Origin of Civil Liberties in the United States* (New York, New York: 1979)

Nash, Margaret. *"How to Be Thankful for Being Free": Searching for a Convergence of Discourses on Teaching Patriotism, Citizenship, and United States History,* Teachers College Record, Volume 107, Number 1 (2005)

National Association of State Boards of Education. *Any Time, Any Place, Any Path, Any Pace, Taking the Lead on e-Learning Policy* (Washington, D.C.: 2001)

National Center for Education Progress Assessment on Educational Progress,

United States Department of Education. *The Nation's Report Card* (Washington, D.C.)

The National Conference on Citizenship in Association with Center for Information and Research on Civic Learning and Engagement (CIRCLE) and Saguaro Seminar. *America's Civic Health Index, Broken Engagement* (Washington, D.C.: 2006)

Neal, Anne and Martin, Jerry; American Council of Trustees and Alumni. *Losing America's Memory, Historical Illiteracy in the 21st Century* (Washington, D.C.: 2000)

Neal, Anne and Martin, Jerry; American Council of Trustees and Alumni. *Restoring America's Legacy* (Washington, D.C.: 2002)

Noveck, Joceyln. *AP Tries Ban to Find Out If We Need Paris,* The Oakland Press (March 2, 2007)

Oates, Stephen. *With Malice Toward None: A Life of Abraham Lincoln* (New York, New York: 1994)

Obama, Barack. *Selma Voting Rights March Commemoration* (March, 2007)

www.oll.libertyfund.org

Oritsejafor, Emmanuel and Guseh, James. *Civic Education Among College Students: A Case Study* (North Carolina Central University: Undated)

Our Nation's Archive, The History of the United States in Documents (Erik Bruun and Jay Crosby, eds) (New York, New York: 1999)

Padover, Saul. *To Secure These Blessings* (New York, New York: 1962)

Paine, Thomas. *The Essential Thomas Paine* (Sidney Hook, ed) (New York, New York: 1969)

Palmer, R. R. *The World of the French Revolution* (New York, New York: 1971)

www.patriotresource.com

A Patriot's Handbook, Song, Poems, Stories and Speeches Celebrating the Land We Love (Caroline Kennedy, ed) (New York, New York: 2003)

Peterson, Merrill. *Thomas Jefferson & the New Nation* (New York, New York: 1970)

Pittinsky, T.L., Rosenthal, S.A., Bacon, L.M., Montoya, R.M., and Zhu, W.; Center for Public Leadership, John F. Kennedy School of Government, Harvard University. *National Leadership Index 2006: A National Study of Confidence in Leadership* (Cambridge, Massachusetts: 2006)

Rembar, Charles. *The Law of the Land, The Evolution of Our Legal System* (New York, New York: 1989)

Rush, Benjamin. *The Selected Writings of Benjamin Rush* (Dagobert Runes, ed) (New York, New York: 1947)

Schama, Simon. *Citizens, A Chronicle of the French Revolution* (New York, New York: 1989)

Smith, Tom and Kim, Seokho; National Opinion Research Center/University of Chicago. *National Pride in Cross-National and Temporal Perspective,* International Journal of Public Opinion Research, 18 (Spring, 2006)

Sources of the American Mind, A Collection of Documents and Texts in American Intellectual History (Loren Baritz, ed) (New York, New York: 1966)

Sources of Our Liberties, Documentary Origins of Individual Liberties in the United States Constitution and Bill of Rights (Special Edition) (Richard Perry & John Cooper, eds) (Chicago, Illinois: 1990)

The Spirit of 'Seventy-Six, The Story of the American Revolution as Told by Participants (Henry Steel Commager and Richard Morris, eds) (Indianapolis, Indiana: 1958)

Stern, Sheldon; Thomas B. Fordham Institute. *Effective State Standards for U.S. History: A 2003 Report Card* (Washington, D.C.: 2003)

Story, Joseph. *Commentaries on the Constitution of the United States; With a Preliminary Review of the Constitutional History of the Colonies and States, Before the Adoption of the Constitution* (Boston, Massachusetts: 1833)

Sydenham, M.J., *The French Revolution* (New York, New York: 1965)

Thomas B. Fordham Foundation. *Where Did Social Studies Go Wrong?* (James Leming, Lucien Ellington, and Kathleen Porter-Magee, eds) (Washington, D.C.: 2003)

Tocqueville, Alexis de. *Democracy in America, Specially Edited and Abridged for the Modern Reader* (Richard D. Heffner, ed) (New York, New York: 1984 (originally published (1835))

Trenchard, John and Gordon, Thomas. *Cato's Letters or Essays on Liberty, Civil and Religious, and Other Important Subjects* (Ronald Hamowy, ed) (Indianapolis, Indiana: 1995 (originally published 1720-1723))

United States Senate, Committee on the Judiciary, Report (June 7, 1937)

Urofsky, Melvin. *A March of Liberty, A Constitutional History of the United States* (New York, New York: 1988)

Warren, Earl. *The Public Papers of Chief Justice Earl Warren* (Henry Christman, ed) (New York, New York: 1959)

Warren, Michael. *Celebrate U.S. System of Freedom, Equal Rights*, The Detroit News (September, 2002)

Warren, Michael. *Keep 'America' in Michigan Schools, State Bureaucrats Want To Do What Stalin, Osama Could Only Dream About*, The Detroit News (May 24, 2006)

Washington, George. *George Washington, A Collection* (W. B. Allen, ed) (Indianapolis, Indiana: 1988)

Watkins, Thomas. *Exploring E-Learning Reforms for Michigan, The New Education (R)evolution* (Detroit, Michigan: 2005), http://www.coe.wayne.edu/elearningReport.pdf

West, Thomas. *Vindicating the Founders, Race, Sex, Class, and Justice in the Origins of America* (Lanham, Maryland: 2001)

Wills, Garry. *Lincoln at Gettysburg* (New York, New York: 1992)

Wood, Gordon S. *Creation of the American Republic, 1776-1787* (New York, New York: 1972)

Wood, Gordon S. *The Radicalism of the American Revolution* (New York, New York: 1993)

Wright, Esmond. *Fabric of Freedom, 1763-1800* (New York, New York: 1964)

Index

D

E

F

G

J

K

L

M

About The Author

Michael Warren serves as an Oakland County Michigan Circuit Court Judge. He is a former member of the Michigan State Board of Education, and currently serves on several nonprofit boards, including the Michigan Center for Civic Education, the Michigan Council for Economics Education, and The New Common School Foundation. He received The Great Influence Award from the Michigan Council for the Social Studies, and a Special Tribute from the Michigan Legislature. Judge Warren has published many articles, commentaries, and editorials regarding education and legal reform.

To order additional copies of America's Survival Guide and for more information about our First Principles, American history, current events, and Judge Warren's recommendations regarding education, legal, holiday, media, nonprofit, and political reform, visit: www.AmericasSurvivalGuide. com.

Printed in the United States
110759LV00001B/187-207/A